THE ATHLETE'S COOKBOOK

THE FAVORITE RECIPES
OF RED BULL ATHLETES,
PREPARED AT HANGAR-7

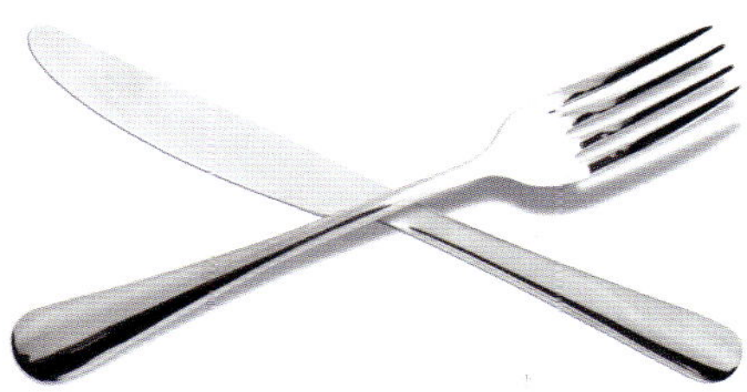

Schiffer Publishing Ltd®

4880 Lower Valley Road • Atglen, PA 19310

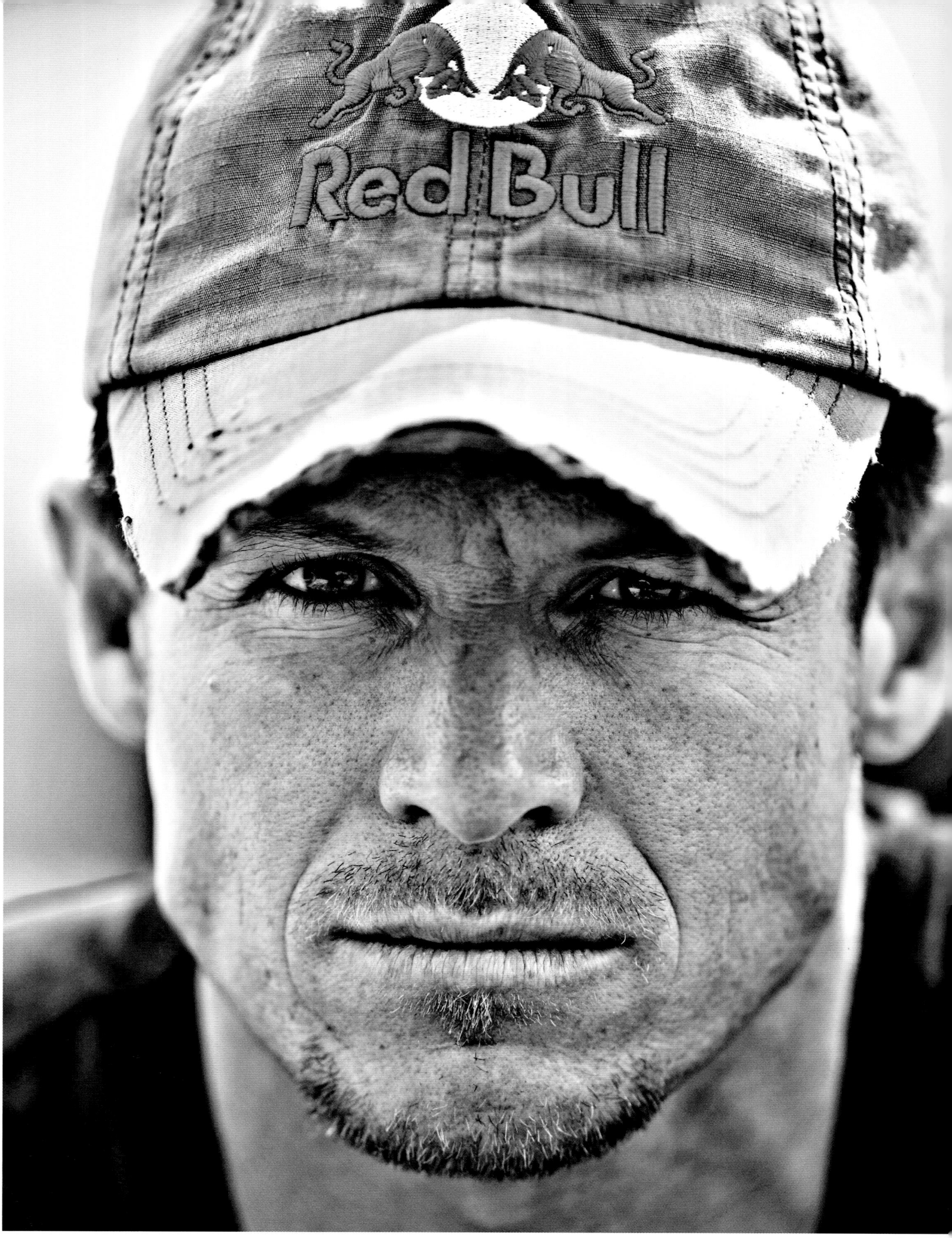
Red Bull

DEAR COOKS AND THOSE WHO REFUSE TO COOK.

Naturally my buddy Roland Trettl asked me as well whether I wanted to prepare my favorite meal with him for the *Red Bull Athlete's Cookbook*.
I thought about it for some time. There are a lot of dishes I enjoy. But which one of them should I cook?

In the end I declined. The fastest man in the world, wearing an apron, standing in front of a stove? No, somehow that wasn't right. I admit that cooking is not among my favorite activities, nor is it one of my fortes, to put it mildly. And as everybody should stick to what he or she does well and what is fun, I stayed on the other side of the table, as a good eater.

When looking over the dishes I can well imagine one or the other on my plate. And perhaps, but only perhaps, there will come a time when I will grab a pot and prepare one of the recipes of this book. Before that I will ask Roland which one I should choose. After all, for me, things have to be fast.

Have fun with my athlete colleagues and their favorite dishes!

Felix Baumgartner

INDICATOR LABELS ON THE PATH TO A LEGEND.

You should know these icons before starting with the *Red Bull Athlete's Cookbook*.

The alarm clock shows you how long the athlete needs to prepare the dish as a guideline for you at home.

The scale from 1 to 10 indicates how difficult it is to prepare the dish.

The section "The long way to the top" provides simple tips and tricks from the repertoire of the master chef.

Note: All of the recipes and quantities in this cookbook are based on serving 4 people.

HANNES ARCH

ACROBATIC AND STUNT PILOT

Roast beef steak with lamb's lettuce salad and Styrian pumpkin seed vinaigrette

BJØRN DUNKERBECK

WINDSURFER

Grilled salmon with vegetables and wild rice

NATASCHA BADMANN

TRIATHLETE

Chickpea bread with salad

ORLANDO DUQUE

CLIFF DIVER

Hawaiian-style poke

PETER BESENYEI

AEROBATIC PILOT

Rakott Krumpli

MARKUS EDER

FREESTYLE SKIER

South Tyrolian spinach-cheese gnocchi with bacon-coleslaw

50 - 57

MATTIAS EKSTRÖM
RACECAR DRIVER

Fusilli Bolognese à la Ekström

58 - 63

STEFAN GLOWACZ
PROFESSIONAL MOUNTAINEER
AND EXTREME CLIMBER

Veal cheeks with rocket salad polenta and oven vegetables

64 - 71

MARIO GÓMEZ
SOCCER PLAYER

Bison tatar
with potato-rösti

72 - 79

ROMAN HAGARA & HANS-PETER STEINACHER
SAILORS

Beetroot soup with horseradish cream
Zander filet with mashed potatoes and leek vegetables

80 - 85

MARCEL HIRSCHER
ALPINE SKIER

Sausage salad with home fries

86 - 93

KARINA HOLLEKIM
B.A.S.E. JUMPER & FREESTYLE SKIER

Tuna Thai-style

94 - 99

JANA DUKATOVÁ & VAVRINEC HRADILEK
KAYAKERS & CANOEISTS

Euro-Mexican wraps

100 - 105

MARC JANKO
SOCCER PLAYER

Burgers with Mediterranean potato salad

106 - 111

BENJAMIN KARL
ALPINE SNOWBOARDER

Pepper steak with
potato gratins and porcini

112 - 119

OLGA KHARLAN
FENCER

Borscht

120 - 125

DAVID LAMA
CLIMBER

Trout with two kinds of apple

126 - 131

SERGIO LAYOS
BMX RACER

Gazpacho

132 - 137

AKSEL LUND SVINDAL
ALPINE SKIER

Green Thai curry

138 - 143

AXEL NAGLICH
SKI MOUNTAINEER

Creamy crayfish soup

144 - 149

MARIANA PAJÓN
BMX RACER

Ajiaco con Pollo

150 - 159

MICHAL PROKOP & MARTIN SONKA
BMX & MOUNTAINBIKE RACER
AEROBATIC PILOT

Chicken burger/Steak burger

160 - 167

GREGOR SCHLIERENZAUER
SKI JUMPER

Roasted suckling and
pork belly with potato-parsley dumplings,
radish-apple salad and mushrooms

168 - 179

DANIEL SERRA & FELIPE FRAGA

RACECAR DRIVERS

Spaghetti al Pomodoro

180 - 185

JORDY SMITH

SURFER

Bunny chow

186 - 191

MARKUS STÖCKL

EXTREME BIKER

Carame ized pan-fried apples

192 - 201

MATTHIAS TRATTNIG & ALEXANDER BARTA

ICE HOCKEY PLAYERS

Sushi

202 - 209

ROLAND TRETTL

COOK

Vinaigrette

210 - 215

BEITSKE VISSER

RACECAR DRIVER

Wortelschotel

216 - 221

LINDSEY VONN

ALPINE SKIER

Linzer cake meets banana bread

222 - 227

MARK WEBBER

RACECAR DRIVER

Chili pasta with
shrimp and cherry toma:oes

Red Bull

"EVERYONE HAS HIS LIMITS; NOT EVERYONE ACCEPTS THEM."

[RED BULL ATHLETES]

These words of Felix Baumgartner have inspired millions of people. With Red Bull Stratos, the B.A.S.E. jumper has demonstrated that one can make their dreams come true, even if everyone else at first thinks you are crazy.

However, this quote might as well have come from BMX racer Mariana Pajón, who fulfilled her dream of Olympic gold at the London Games. And from Gregor Schlierenzauer, who is the most successful ski jumper of all time at twenty-three. Or from surfer legend Bjørn Dunkerbeck, who has won everything but still has a goal for the future.

In other words, this phrase might actually come from any of the over 600 Red Bull athletes who overcome limits in their sport behind which their dreams are hidden.

Because whatever motivates them is worth it and inspires other people—perhaps, one day, millions of them.

WHERE HIGH FLYERS LAND.

[HANGAR-7 & IKARUS RESTAURANT]

The world of Red Bull doesn't fit under a roof. How could it? By now it would have to include the stratosphere. But a center for the world of Red Bull, that is entirely possible. A location with a pulse 365 days a year, where people feel at ease—people who by their very nature want to go further, be it on the racing track, the skatepark, or on stage.

For this reason, since 2003, there is Hangar-7 in Salzburg. This building does not have a roof that encloses a small universe, but one that opens towards a new, big world.

The culinary part of Hangar-7 follows this concept. For this reason, it is not only a master chef cooking at the Ikarus Restaurant. The best cooks in the world cook here; every month a different one. The patron of this international unique culinary project is master chef Eckart Witzigmann.

The executive chef is Roland Trettl. His job as part of this book is to provide even more wings for the Red Bull athletes from where he can do it best: at the stove.

HANGAR-7 IKARUS DAS RESTAURANT

AS LONG AS SUPPLIES LAST.

It's gotten late. Eyes are small and hunger is huge. Go grocery shopping? Sure, if there was one still open. Gas station? None nearby. So check out what the pantry has to offer.

This is the moment of truth: are there at least some scrambled eggs? Or just a long face?

All or nothing—this can be taken care of with a small amount of supplies that should be part of every kitchen.

Compiled by Roland Trettl.

BREAD
TOASTBROT
LAUREL LEAVES
BREADCRUMBS
SEMMELBRÖSEL
E BALSAMIC VINEGAR
WEISSER BALSAMICO
DRIED CHILI
SUNFLOWER OIL
SONNEN-BLUMENÖL
CHOCOLATE
SCHOKOLADE
SEA SALT
MEERSALZ
WHOLE MILK
VOLLMILCH
CRANBERRIES
PREISELBEEREN
SOUR CREAM
SAUERRAHM
BUTTER
MARMELADE
STRAWBERRIES
ERDBEEREN
EGGS
PARSLEY
ROSEMARY
SOY SAUCE
PEPPERONI
PICKLES
HORSERADISH
OBERSKREN
SOJASAUCE
CAPERS
KAPERN
Kaviar
OLIVES
CHAMPAGNE
Sekt
SAUSAGE
CHEESE
CHEESE
TOMATO PASTE
BACON
CUCUMBER
TOMATOES
CHERRY TOMATOES
BELL PEPPER
EGGPLANT
STEAK
AVOCADO
GARLIC
ONIONS
CHICKEN
BASIL
BEER
POTATOES
SCALLIONS
BIER
CARPE DIEM
KOMBUCHA
CLASSIC

AEROBATIC AND
STUNT PILOT

AUSTRIA
RESIDENCE: SALZBURG

HANNES ARCH

STYRIAN EXTREME.

NAME: Hannes Arch

BIRTHDAY: September 22, 1967

HEIGHT: 1.80 m (5' 9½")

WEIGHT: 79 kg (174 lbs)

HOBBIES: climbing, B.A.S.E. jumping

WEBSITE: www.hannesarch.com

TWITTER: @HannesArch

On his homepage Hannes Arch describes himself as an "allround adventurer." Although "adventurer" might be the wrong term. "Crazy" would be more fitting, in the best sense of the word. The athlete who grew up in Styria and lives in Salzburg is attracted to the extremes like a moth toward a light.

As a B.A.S.E. jumper, he created a huge stir with his jump from the massive Eiger north face. With the Red Bull X-Alps he invented "the world's toughest adventure race, where the participants have to use nothing but their legs and the paraglider to conquer 1,000 kilometers (621 miles) of the Alps. And as an aerobatic pilot he has shaped the Red Bull Air Race—among other things, obtaining the world championship in 2008.

2006
European freestyle champion

2008
Red Bull world champion Air Race World Series

2009
Vice world champion Red Bull Air Race World Series

2010
Vice world champion Red Bull Air Race World Series

2012
Bronze medal at the FAI European Aerobatic World Championships, freestyle

"I KNOW FEAR ONLY FROM THEORY."

Daredevil and high flyer: Hannes Arch is where adventure is.

KETCHUP IS ALWAYS A MUST.

[INTERVIEW]

WHAT MAKES YOUR DISCIPLINED ATHLETE'S HEART BECOME WEAK? AND WHAT WOULD YOU NEVER PICK UP WITH A FORK?

No matter whether salad, pasta, or meat, ketchup is always a must. It's funny, I actually don't like beer that much.

WHAT WAS YOUR MOST IMPORTANT BAD DECISION REGARDING NUTRITION BEFORE OR DURING A COMPETITION?

I am fine with everything, so this is not a problem for me.

AND WHAT WAS THE CRAZIEST THING YOU EVER ATE?

When I was in Korea they actually served me live squid. I ate it (laughs).

WHAT ARE THE EVENINGS AND MORNINGS BEFORE A COMPETITION LIKE? WHAT DO YOU PUT ON YOUR PLATE AND INTO YOUR GLASS?

In the morning a Bircher Müsli is mandatory, with as much yogurt as possible. After that I only eat energy bars and drink water.

WHAT'S INSIDE YOUR FREEZER?

Leek strudel made by my mom—that one always has to be there. Then there is homemade bread. And spices.

HOW DO YOU CELEBRATE A SUCCESSFUL COMPETITION?

With a glass of Styrian white wine.

YOU HAVE ONE LAST MEAL. WHAT WOULD YOU ORDER?

I simply indulge without limits! (laughs). Pumpkin cream soup, lamb's salad with potatoes and pumpkin seed oil, a steak with potato gratin, pasta arrabiata, and some tiramisu for dessert. And a bottle of plum brandy to go with it.

A LOOK INTO THE CRYSTAL BALL: WHAT COMES AFTER YOUR CAREER—MORE SIXPACK ABS OR A BACON-WRAPPED SIX PACK?

More like a bacon-wrapped six pack.

COOKING IS ...

... an art of which I understand very little. And a sensitivity which I don't have—not yet.

THE LONG WAY TO THE TOP

CAESAR'S BOWL.

The ancient Romans knew how to cook really well, and for this reason they invented the mortar. A container named after the Latin word *mortari* for crushing, it can be utilized for crushing plants, spices, nuts, or seeds with the help of a pestle. This method is still relevant in the kitchen, even after 2,000 years. "It simply results in a much better and more intense taste when compared to cutting up the ingredients with a knife," says Roland Trettl.

ROAST BEEF STEAK

WITH LAMB'S LETTUCE SALAD AND STYRIAN PUMPKIN SEED VINAIGRETTE

25
MINUTES

DIFFICULTY SCALE
4

INGREDIENTS:
- 3–4 red onions
- 1 garlic clove
- olive oil
- salt
- pepper
- 1 sprig of thyme
- 1 sprig of rosemary
- 400 g (14 oz) roast beef
- 30 g (1¼ oz) lamb's lettuce
- 10 g (½ oz) fresh porcini mushrooms
- pumpkin seeds

PUMPKIN SEED VINAIGRETTE:
- 50 g (2 oz) pumpkin seeds
- salt (coarse-grained)
- 30 g (1 fl oz) pumpkin seed oil
- 60 g (2 fl oz) young balsamic vinegar
- 10 g (1/3 fl oz) old balsamic vinegar

Wearing a sweater in the kitchen of Ikarus restaurant is not such a great idea to start with. When Rolant Trettl fires up the grill, a swimsuit would be a more adequate outfit. But what was the Ikarus chef supposed to do? After all, his guest —a declared anti-cook—wished for a genuine Styrian dish. And what does that bring to mind: lamb's lettuce, of course. And what goes best with it? Exactly ...

A roast beef steak has to come from the grill, and since the outdoor lounge is closed during autumn, the only option is to light up the charcoal in the kitchen itself. Fortunately, the kitchen on the lower floor of Hangar-7 features a huge extractor.

When Hannes Arch enters the kitchen, the first thing he does is roll up his sleeves, but not only because of the temperature. "If Hannes can't cook too well he might as well be a good assistant," Roland says.

Hannes thinks this is a good deal, and he gets busy peeling onions and garlic for the lamb's salad. "I love onions and garlic," the aerobatic pilot tells his counterpart while cutting the onions into even thin slices. He adds with a laugh:

"Of all things, the items which are problematic in society."

The onion rings are braised together with a few pieces of garlic (which are later removed) in a pan with olive oil and pepper. Thyme and rosemary are also added to the pan. Once the onions are nice and golden, simply turn off the heat and put a plate on the pan to keep them warm.

Roland thinks porcini are the ideal addition to the salad. The privilege of a master chef: just one word and he's got them in front of him. The mushrooms are grated directly into the salad bowl. "Porcini are a real wonder of taste," muses Roland. "But they have to be raw. You should never ever fry them!" Now both of them tackle the vinaigrette: Hannes crushes pumpkin seeds in the mortar. Roland adds coarse salt and a shot of pumpkin seed oil, as well as young and old balsamic vinegar. "The young *aceto balsamico* adds sweetness to the vinaigrette, the old one adds acidity," explains the master chef.

As quickly as things have progressed so far for this dish, the steak doesn't take long, either. The piece of roast beef is rubbed with olive oil on both sides and salt and pepper is added. Hannes places it at the center of the pre-heated grill and roasts it medium. Not even four minutes later it is done and can be prepared.

Roland cuts the roast beef into strips of a few centimeters (an inch). Together with the washed and cleaned salad—which was mixed with the vinaigrette —they are added into the bowl. Finally,

the roasted onions are placed on top and pumpkin seeds are added.

"A great dish," says the master chef, rubbing his hands together, "and incredibly fast to prepare!" And Hannes is blown away after tasting the first bite:

"This looks almost fancy, although we wanted it to be down-to-earth."

A lot of taste with little effort: you don't have to be a kitchen pro for this dish.

TRIATHLETE

SWITZERLAND
RESIDENCE: OFTRINGEN

NATASCHA BADMANN

THE QUEEN OF THE KONA COAST.

NAME: Natascha Badmann

BIRTHDAY: December 6, 1966

HEIGHT: 1.65 m (5' 4")

WEIGHT: 52 kg (114½ lbs)

DISCIPLINE: duathlete and triathlete

HOBBIES: classical music, garden, roses, painting, nature

WEBSITE: www.nataschabadmann.ch

Natascha Badmann describes the 2007 Hawaii Ironman World Championship as like no other competition. It is not a race she will win. Not one where she leaves her competitors behind, as she's done so often. She suffered a serious fall while biking. She briefly lost consciousness but got up again and called for a spare bike (as hers is irreparably damaged) and continued. She wanted to finish the competition, despite the initial diagnosis of a broken collar bone, large skin abrasions, and much pain. Only her trainer and partner Toni Hasler managed to convince her to leave the race. Later it became apparent that several torn muscles, bone fractures, and cartilage damage in the shoulders meant her career was over. Badmann did not believe it. She trained daily and she came back. It is this willpower that has currently made Badmann the world's most successful triathlete.

Natascha discovered the triathlon at twenty-four. Two years later she was among the world's duathlon elite. In 1998, she won the legendary Hawaii Ironman for the first time; five more world championship titles follow this grueling competition. Now forty-six, Badmann is still part of the winner's list of long-distance races. How is this possible? With precise season planning, an always positive attitude, and radiance as well as extreme discipline—including nutrition. And last but not least, an immense willpower.

6 x HAWAII IRONMAN WORLD CHAMPION

2 x HAWAII VICE WORLD CHAMPION
1 x DUATHLON WORLD CHAMPION
1 x DUATHLON EUROPEAN CHAMPION
2 x WINNER OF THE ZOFINGEN POWERMAN
8-TIME WINNER OF THE LONG AND MEDIUM IRONMAN DISTANCE

1998 & 2002

Swiss athlete of the year

RedBull

HAPPY BY NATURE.

[INTERVIEW]

WHICH TWO (STILL LIVING OR HISTORIC) PERSONS ARE SITTING AT YOUR PERFECT DINNER TABLE?

Toni (Note: Toni Hasler is Natascha's trainer and partner). Or Robert Redford—but then I would have to not invite Toni ...

WHICH FAMOUS SPORTSMAN/ SPORTSWOMAN WOULD YOU LIKE TO HAVE DINNER WITH?

Roger Federer, because he has stayed so natural and I find him very likeable. I have known him for many years.

THE TASTE OF YOUR CHILDHOOD IS ...

... rather bitter.

BEER IN THE OUTDOOR GARDEN OR A GLASS OF WINE AT THE BAR?

Red wine. First, it is the only alcohol I drink, and I prefer a cozy and relaxed evening.

WHAT IS THE STRANGEST THING YOU EVER ATE?

There must be many who think that my daily meals are strange. When I am training I eat something every ten minutes.

WHAT WAS IT YOU SIMPLY COULDN'T STAND AS A CHILD? AND DO YOU ENJOY IT TODAY?

Beets and fennel. And I hated lentils. But now I like them so much I can even prepare them myself!

SWEET OR SOUR?

Sweet!

AT THE TABLE WITH FAMILY/FRIENDS: ARE YOU THE FIRST ONE TO FINISH OR DO YOU ENJOY EVERY SINGLE BITE?

I always try to enjoy the food, but after several hours of training the thing is that everybody is done and I am still eating because I have gone for seconds and thirds ...

WHAT DOES A SUCCESSFUL TRIATHLETE HAVE IN COMMON WITH A GOOD COOK?

Passion and perfectionism!

YOU ARE PLANNING A ROMANTIC DINNER FOR TWO: WHERE DOES IT TAKE PLACE?

Inside of a nice garden with roses under a gazebo with candle light. It is nice and warm and one is surrounded by the aromas of nature.

YOU WAKE UP WITH THE MUNCHIES. WHAT IS IN YOUR REFRIGERATOR?

Um, perhaps not in the fridge, but my protein powder has to be nearby at all times. And Red Bull.

TRY TO COMPARE YOUR SPORT WITH A DISH. WHICH ONE COMES TO YOUR MIND?

A curry, because of the variety of tastes that are combined: spicy, sweet, the different colors, the warming chili.

WHERE DOES THE FUN STOP WITH NUTRITION?

With deep-frying and with fast food. That's just filling up, not eating.

COOKING IS ...

... great, and a lot of fun. But eating is better, because at home, Toni is the one who does the cooking!

THE LONG WAY TO THE TOP

DRINKING HEALTH - A SUMMER TEA.

Apart from Red Bull, there are other options to do something good for your body when taking in fluid. For example, with a homemade summer tea à la Badmann: cut one organic lemon (because of the peel) into thin slices, put it into a jug with a handful of fresh elderberry flowers, 30 fresh mint leaves, 6 thin slices of ginger, and some curcumin root, and pour 1.5 liters (50 fl oz) of hot (not boiling!) water over it. Allow it to cool down and put in a cool place. A great thirst quencher, and no sugar!

CHICKPEA BREAD

WITH SALAD

12 HOURS PREPARATION

40 MINUTES

SCALE **4**

INGREDIENTS:
500 g (1 lb 2 oz) chickpeas
1 onion
50 g (1.69 fl oz) olive oil
1 garlic clove
8 eggs
1 pinch of paprika powder
2 celery stalks
1 carrot
1 TBSP chopped parsley
1 TBSP chopped chives
50 g (2 oz) Parmesan cheese
1 pinch of pepper
1 pinch of nutmeg

SALAD & SALAD DRESSING:
1 lettuce
2 shallots
1 salad cucumber
juice of 1/2 lemon
10 radishes
1 piece ginger root
1 piece curcuma (turmeric) root
10 green olives
1 TBSP chopped parsley
1 TBSP chives in small rolls
10 cherry tomatoes
100 g (3 oz) hard tofu (for cutting)
100 g (3 oz) feta cheese
50 g (1.69 fl oz) apple vinegar
4 different oils: linseed oil, olive oil, argan oil and pumpkin seed oil

Roland Trettl actually deserves an award from Brussels because he contributes in a big way to remove the "butter mountains" of the European Union. And the owners of salt mines and salt works should have donated a monument, too (see "The seven commandments of pasta" on page 57).

MEETS:

Natascha Badmann manages her calories like Formula 1 technicians do octane values. With competitions of nine hours and more, training weeks starting at forty hours, and a career of more than seventeen years as a competitive world-class athlete, nutrition is a key to success and a personal philosophy.

Apple or Windows. Celtics or Rangers. Scooter or Vespa. This afternoon there was somewhat of a war of faith on the program in the Ikarus kitchen. Two nutritional philosophies met with much entertainment for everyone present.

Recently in SALT(Z)burg: chickpea bread.

Roland Trettl had prepared things ahead of time. Twelve hours before Natascha's arrival he had soaked the chickpeas in water. Now the second most successful woman in the history of the Hawaii triathlon stands at the stove next to the master chef, filling a pressure cooker with water and then adding the chickpeas with one whole onion. As usual, Roland reaches into his salt container to throw a sizeable quantity into the water when a desperate scream from the Swiss triathlete is heard: "No salt!" Visibly flummoxed, Trettl opens his hand and puts the salt back into the bowl and gets on with the next procedure.

He cuts 1 onion and 1 garlic clove into fine pieces, then walks the cutting board to a pan resting on a stove and adds the olive oil. Natascha's question as to what he is up to is answered by the master chef with a dry "braise them." This time the scream causes him to squirm. "Noooo Roland, no way. After frying there's only fat left over from the oil and you will carry it around for days. No, really, no way." We should now mention that in a kitchen such as the one at Ikarus there is a discipline like in an elite unit. Every command from the chief cook is answered by the entire staff with "Yes, chef." Objections are as rare as pineapples in the Arctic. Roland's disbelieving stare says it all. "Without oil there is no taste. And as a cook I always try to add taste." They agree to briefly braise the onion and garlic in a coated pan, without fat.

Meanwhile, Badmann tosses the eggs into a bowl, adds the drained chickpeas and paprika, and blends it all

with the braised onion and garlic with an immersion blender. Roland's reach for the salt is aptly nipped in the bud and he is asked to pass along the celery and carrots. "This doesn't go into the blender; vegetables must always be finely chopped. Otherwise the taste is lost," counters the chef and cuts the celery and the carrots into tiny cubes. He then chops the parsley and chives, grates the Parmesan, and mixes the herbs and cheese under the blended peas. Natasha works the pepper mill and adds a bit of nutmeg. To Trettl's suggestion to add some salt she replies with a determined shake of her head which causes the cook to laugh again. "Natascha, if I would cook like this every day every guest would go to the hospital for lunch." Now some time is given to allow the dough to rest.

"You are cutting like I do biking with a nice high frequency," Natascha comments about Trettl's quick handling of the blade when he peels the cucumber and then cuts it into slices for the salad. Then he chops shallots, radishes, parsley, and olives. A few finely sliced pieces of ginger follow, as well as half a root of turmeric. The South Tyrolian mixes everything inside a bowl and adds two tablespoons each of olive oil, linseed oil, pumpkin seed oil, and argan oil over the marinade.

The salad.

He then slices the cherry tomatoes and chops the tofu and feta cheese into small cubes, then adds them to the other ingredients. Now add the juice of half a lemon and a tablespoon of apple vinegar and pour the marinade over the lettuce. Mix everything once again. Natascha doesn't leave anything to chance, or to Roland Trettl when it comes to frying, and has placed herself first in line right in front of the pan. Now both chefs shape small flat breads from the pea dough which Badmann carefully places inside the pan, where a dash of oil is noticeable. She fries the breads on

Frying the breads: the fight about oil.

very low heat to, as she says, prevent the oil from becoming toxic. Roland is standing next to her and mischievously remarks that he would have done exactly like her, only with more oil and more salt. He shrugs and puts the salad into deep plates and places the first golden-brown chickpea bread onto the green leaves.

Dinner is ready. Before Trettl takes the first bite Natascha explains to him why this is the perfect meal for her. This dish contains everything her body needs after a long day of training: higher-quality proteins than those of meat, carbohydrates, vitamins, and high-quality oils that are important for cell

The finish: tastes great or doesn't?

regeneration. And she also mentions the topic of salt once again. With competitions under extreme climatic conditions such as in Hawaii, details matter. If the body uses too much salt because it is used to taking up a lot of it, the race can be over quickly. Trettl has already started eating, but he nods and shows comprehension. For Badmann's requirements everything makes sense. Then he puts the eating utensils aside and gets up. Accompanied by Natascha's questioning look, "I'm just picking up some salt. That's the good thing about it, you can always add it later."

"The orders here remind me of the Energy Lab at the Hawaii Ironman at about kilometer 30 (mile 18). The US Marine Corps does duty at the refreshment post. When I get there I always shout what I want, **"Water, ice, coke!" And the soldier always runs next to me, hands me the items, and screams: "Yes Mam! Water, ice, coke, Mam!"**

Trettl about the experience of healthy cooking: "It certainly makes sense for an endurance machine like Natascha, but if I had to cook like this for two weeks I would become depressed."

AEROBATIC PILOT

HUNGARY
RESIDENCE: HERCEGHALOM

PETER BESENYEI

SIMPLY LEGEND-AIRY.

NAME: Peter Besenyei

BIRTHDAY: June 8, 1956

HEIGHT: 1.85 m (6' 1")

WEIGHT: 73 kg (161 lbs)

HOBBIES: sky diving, car racing, photography, fishing, skiing, music

WEBSITE: www.besenyeipeter.hu

Peter Besenyei is what you call a legend. The Hungarian won his first competition at twenty with a glider, and during the following three decades, he became one of the world's best aerobatic pilots. This is proven with two world championships and as many World Grand Prix titles. At the beginning of the new millennium, he took the control stick of his sport into his own hands, leading him to new heights as the "architect" of the Red Bull Air Race, in which he takes part as a pilot. Always with him is his prominent bar above the upper lip—depending on his shaving mood, adorned with a full beard—which Peter Besenyi guides as unerringly through all of the fashion trends as he has his machines for the past thirty years.

Atoll daredevil: Peter Besenyei over the Kaafu Atoll in the Maldive Islands.

1995
European freestyle and mandatory program champion

1998
1. place
FAI World Grand Prix

2000
World Champion freestyle

2001
1. place
FAI World Grand Prix

2005
Vice world champion
Red Bull Air Race World Series

2006
Vice world champion
Red Bull Air Race World Series

2007
3. place
Red Bull Air Race World Series

"I NEVER RISK MY NECK. EVER!"

Gigantic: during an air show in Sri Lanka Peter Besenyei visits the Sigiriya Rock —from above, of course.

A SMILE AND A GLASS OF WINE.

[INTERVIEW]

WHAT MAKES YOUR DISCIPLINED ATHLETE'S HEART BECOME WEAK? WHAT DO YOU NEVER PICK UP WITH A FORK?

As a pilot I can eat anything, and I do. There is no dish that I don't like—as long as it doesn't taste artificial. I love fish and seafood, and I wouldn't say no to good pasta either. But even frogs and scorpions have made it onto my plate.

WHAT DO THE EVENING AND THE MORNING BEFORE A COMPETITION LOOK LIKE IN YOUR CASE? WHAT'S ON YOUR PLATE AND IN YOUR GLASS?

This is always different and depends on the kind of competition. Is it the Air Race, a flying exhibition, or is it a simple classic flight? Before an Air Race I always drink Red Bull. I don't say this because they are my sponsor, but because it actually helps to keep up concentration.

HOW DO YOU CELEBRATE A SUCCESSFUL COMPETITION?

With a smile and a glass of wine. But it happens rarely where I say to myself after a competition: "This was perfect." And if so I have rarely won, strangely enough.

THE TASTE OF YOUR CHILDHOOD IS ...

... honey. No matter whether in milk or on bread with some butter, I could always eat honey by the ton.

YOU HAVE A FREE LAST MEAL. WHAT WOULD YOU ORDER?

Seafood—best would be a crab. And of course a glass of wine.

WHITE OR RED?

I don't have rules here. There are a whole lot of great Hungarian wines. And I like Chilean reds and white wines from New Zealand.

WHICH CHARACTERISTIC UNITES A SUCCESSFUL AEROBATIC PILOT WITH A GOOD COOK?

Not just one characteristic, but there are several things that are crucial both in sports and at the stove: motivation, training, ambition, and precision down to the minute details.

WHICH FAMOUS SPORTSMAN/ SPORTSWOMAN WOULD YOU LIKE TO SHARE A MEAL WITH?

Well, I've gone through all of the sportsmen (laughs). But I'd love to have dinner with Vangelis. He is my absolute favorite musician and composer.

THE LONG WAY TO THE TOP

FOOD ALSO NEEDS REST.

The rule of thumb for a soufflé: it tastes best on the second day. Not only grandma says so, but a master chef as well. If you leave the dish to rest in the fridge during the night, the resulting gravy is absorbed and the taste can fully develop. So a soufflé is best prepared the day before its intended consumption.

RAKOTT KRUMPLI

90 MINUTES

SCALE **3**

INGREDIENTS:
1 kg (2 lbs) potatoes (mealy-cooking)
salt
4 eggs
4 onions
2–3 apples
4 Frankfurter/Vienna sausages
100 g (3½ oz) hard-cured sausage (e.g. chorizo)
100 g (3½ oz) pork belly
1 sprig of rosemary
1 sprig of thyme
sage
tarragon
corn oil
paprika powder
800 g (28 oz) sour cream
parsley

Few guests have stepped into Hangar-7 with an ice box under their arm and Roland Trettl first has to swallow—more so once the executive chief of Ikarus restaurant sees the contents that Peter Besenyei places on the work counter with a satisfied look on his face.

Frankfurter sausages packed in style in plastic and a piece of pork belly you could knock out a person with. For this meeting Peter Besenyei has plundered the supermarket around the corner—he even brought his own soufflé dish.

"You've brought along an entire kitchen," laughs Roland Trettl while working the controls of the oven: "180 degrees (350°F)?" "Better 200 (400°F)," replies Peter Besenyei. This is the moment when this experienced master chef knows today he won't be the teacher but the apprentice. As a matter of fact, when preparing his "Rakott Krumpli"—loosely translated this means "piled-up potatoes"—this down-to-earth Hungarian relies mainly on one thing: his personal experience at the stove back at home. "It's based on a Hungarian dish, but I've improvised quite a bit."

spices such as rosemary, thyme, sage, and tarragon, and now he grinds them up in the mortar to make a uniquely aromatic blend.

"Man, this is hard work," Peter snorts. "I think we need some wine." And just like that the content of his travel bag is emptied. He decants a bottle of his favorite Hungarian red and Roland takes care of water and glasses: "Cheers!"

The as-yet-empty soufflé dish is rubbed with some corn oil so things don't stick to it. Inside are put about half of the following ingredients: first the potato slices, which receive some paprika powder. Now the onions, Frankfurter, apples, pork belly, sausage, and eggs in this order, and as irregularly as possible. Salt is added to this blend, as well as spices. Then the sour cream. How much, exactly? Peter Besenyi: "There's the real chef speaking." Trettl is excited. "I might invite you as a guest chef of the Ikarus."

"It depends on your gut feeling. And on how much wine you've had."

Trust is okay, control is better: Peter Besenyei looks over Roland Trettl's shoulder with a keen eye.

masterpiece is cut. While the master chef is completely floored—"I am really astonished how good it tastes!"—the expectations of the Air Race pilot are apparently a bit more elevated. "At home it tastes even better," Peter laughs. "But for your first try it is quite good!"

While the potatoes are boiling soft in the saltwater and the eggs hard-boil the two of them get to work on the toughest part of this dish. Onions, apples, Frankfurter, sausage, pork belly, and finally potatoes and the cold-shocked eggs (in ice water)—all of it has to be peeled and finely chopped. Anyhow, this is where Roland can impress his customer with speed and precision. And in matters concerning spices, the Ikarus chef also has the upper hand. He has previously prepared typical Provenzal

Now it's the second layer's turn, which is composed just like the first one. Then all of it goes into the oven. By the way sour cream on top is sufficient. Peter and Roland agree that the intense taste of cheese would destroy everything. Furthermore, the executive chef suggests refining the sour cream with horseradish, but he can't quite convince the pilot.

After a good half an hour the Rakott Krumpli à la Besenyei is done. Roland adds some parsley, then the

Mission accomplished: Peter takes a photo to show back home.

WINDSURFER

NETHERLANDS/DENMARK
RESIDENCE: LAS PALMAS DE GRAN CANARIA, SPAIN

BJØRN DUNKERBECK

A COSMOPOLITAN ON THE WAVE OF SUCCESS.

NAME: Bjørn Dunkerbeck

NICKNAME: Dunki

BIRTHDAY: July 16, 1969

HEIGHT: 1.91 m (6' 2½")

WEIGHT: 104 kg (229 lbs)

DISCIPLINE: slalom, speed, wave

HOBBIES: surfing, MTB, snowboarding

WEBSITE: www.dunkerbeck.com

For Bjørn, the son of Danish-Dutch parents who grew up in Spain the term home has always been a flexible thing.

When "Dunki" first got onto a surfboard at nine his main residence from that moment on became the water. Forty-one world champion titles not only make him a figurehead of windsurfing, but also one of the world's best athletes.

And so, being in his mid-forties, he could retreat to his home on the Canary Islands and sit happily in his rocking chair and polish his trophies and medals. But this would not be Dunkerbeck's thing, and then there is another big project driving the father of four: "To crack 50 knots on the surfboard before someone else does it."

12 X PWA OVERALL WORLD CHAMPION 88/89/90/91/92/93/94/95/96/97/98/99
5 X PWA COURSE RACING WORLD CHAMPION 90/91/92/93/94
5 X PWA RACING WORLD CHAMPION 95/96/97/98/99
9 X PWA SLALOM WORLD CHAMPION 88/89/90/91/92/93/94/05/11
7 X PWA WAVE WORLD CHAMPION 90/92/93/94/95/99/01
1 X PWA FREESTYLE WORLD CHAMPION 98
2 X ISA SPEED WORLD CHAMPION 94/05

Bjørn has celebrated over 100 victories in the PWA Worldcup and is the only windsurfer with 41 titles in the various disciplines.

Freestyle, wave, and speed: Bjørn Dunkerbeck sets the standards in each discipline.

LAMB FOR THE PARTY, SOUP FOR THE FAREWELL.

[INTERVIEW]

WHEN DOES YOUR DISCIPLINED ATHLETE'S HEART BECOME WEAK?

When I fire up the grill with friends in the summer it has to be really hearty. Without a huge T-bone steak or half a lamb, no deal.

WHAT IS IT YOU NEVER PICK UP WITH A FORK?

Entrails.

WHAT WAS YOUR GREATEST FAUX PAS AS TO NUTRITION, EITHER BEFORE OR DURING A COMPETITION?

Usually I don't eat before surfing. But I once made some calamari with garlic. That wasn't such a great idea …

WHAT IS THE EVENING AND THE MORNING BEFORE A COMPETITION LIKE FOR YOU? WHAT'S ON YOUR PLATE AND IN YOUR GLASS?

As I said, I don't eat before the competition. But in the meantime you need something to give you power. In my case it's usually juice shakes.

HOW DO YOU CELEBRATE A SUCCESSFUL COMPETITION?

Back in those days it might have been quite extreme. But after twenty-five years where you stand on the podium at almost every competition, partying calms down a bit. Today I get a lot out of a cozy dinner with my family.

DO YOU HAVE A FAVORITE RESTAURANT?

Since I travel a lot I happen to know good cooks all over the world. I usually pay them a visit when I am around the area.

YOU HAVE ONE LAST MEAL. WHAT WOULD YOU ORDER?

I am a positive person and I believe I will get to be 100 or older with healthy food, so my last meal would probably be some soup (laughs).

A LOOK INTO THE CRYSTAL BALL: WHAT COMES AFTER YOUR CAREER—MORE SIXPACK ABS OR A SIX PACK WITH BACON WRAP?

I don't even know which sport to practice first when surfing is not my profession anymore, so I am not worried about that.

THE LONG WAY TO THE TOP

FAT FLAVOR CARRIERS.

A fish filet should always be cooked on its skin side as long as possible. This will take longer, but it is more gentle and enhances the taste. This causes the fats—the important flavor carriers—to remain longer in the fish and they can better develop.

GRILLED SALMON

WITH VEGETABLES AND WILD RICE

50
MINUTES

SCALE
5

INGREDIENTS:

4 salmon filets (about 160 g [5-6 oz] each)
1 zucchini
1 red onion
1 eggplant
3 artichokes
1 fennel
300 g (10½ oz) button squash/pumpkin
250 g (9 oz) wild rice
salt
pepper
thyme
1/2 lemon
olive oil

If you disregard the fact that Roland Trettl prefers frozen water sports—the master chef is also a gifted ice hockey player—he has more in common with Bjørn Dunkerbeck than one would at first suspect. Both of them are full-blooded dads, both have remained real sonny boys, and, most importantly, both of them really know how to cook.

How well does Dunkerbeck know the craft at the stove? Well, Trettl gets a taste of it while they discuss a recipe. The fact that it is a fish dish is not very surprising, given the fact we are dealing with a surf legend who lives on the Canary Islands. But the intensity of his involvement is.

In the case of Dunkerbeck, everything is tuned to his personal requirements—more specifically, to his blood type.

"It is really fascinating how differently people can react to one and the same dish," explains the surfer. "And it all has to do with the blood type. For example, orange juice: if I have some in the morning I can forget about the entire day. Another person gets all his energy from it."

"Crazy." Trettl is baffled, "you never stop learning." The master chef and the surf legend on the same wavelength—the best conditions for a great dish.

So they are ready to go:

Trettl triumphantly unpacks a 3.5 kilo (8 lb) monster of a salmon and adds mischieveously: "Of course, ready-made filets are fine, too. But since I got a fresh delivery from Norway I thought you could show off your skills at filleting."

Nice try, Roland! But someone as experienced as Bjørn is not rattled. He cuts up the salmon with precise movements, removes the bones, and then calmly and contently cuts up two large, thick pieces: in the case of a soccer player you would call it a perfect counterattack with a brilliant finish. For Dunkerbeck, this means that someone has gained the upper hand in an impressive way.

Power food: "This dish provides protein and power!"

"Today we are having portions for grown-ups!"

Bjørn might as well keep the knife in his hand to prepare the side dish, because the vegetable rice—as the name suggests—requires quite a bit of vegetables. And they first have to be shaped the right way and chopped. So Bjørn and Roland start chopping up zucchini, onions, eggplant, artichokes, and fennel.

Furthermore, the master chef has thought about how to improve the recipe and he now presents button squash to Bjørn: small, round, and bright yellow plants that not only remind you of pumpkins, they are pumpkins. Hence, Roland explains, you might as well pick a "normal" pumpkin in case you don't have a vegetable market around the corner.

The button squash are cut into small pieces and placed on the griddle, where they are braised together with the other vegetables.

At this point the wild rice should be cooked, and after a few minutes it is mixed with the vegetables and seasoned with salt, pepper, and some thyme. For the perfect taste Roland adds the juice of half a lemon over the vegetable rice.

Now all that is required are the salmon fillets. They are salted and also grilled on the griddle with olive oil. First on the skin side for some ten minutes, then Roland turns them around for a few seconds on the flesh side—and done, one of the fastest dishes in the history of the Ikarus.

By the way: if you don't have a professional kitchen at home, no problem. "You can do this with normal pans," says Roland. "Or you might want to buy a cooking stone," Bjørn interjects. "You can get them at a low price from retailers or on the internet."

Blood type principle: Bjørn shows the book he uses to manage his entire nutrition to Roland.

CLIFFDIVER

COLOMBIA
RESIDENCE: LAIE, HAWAII

ORLANDO DUQUE

FROM GÄNSERNDORF TO THE TOP OF THE WORLD.

NAME: Orlando Duque

NICKNAME: The Duke

BIRTHDAY: September 11, 1974

HEIGHT: 1.75 m (5' 8¾")

WEIGHT: 70 kg (154 lbs)

HOBBIES: bodysurfing, canoeing

Twitter: @orlandoduque

It is a somewhat more gripping variation of the cliché "from dishwasher to millionaire" story. When Orlando Duque dropped out of university in Colombia and made his passion his profession, he at first only found a job at a show in a safari park in Gänserndorf, a small village on the outskirts of Vienna.

But as he quickly became bored jumping from a twenty-five-meter (82 ft) crane into a burning pool Orlando joined the cliff-diving scene, which at that time was just starting out, and became its first poster boy. Today his career is lined with several world championship titles and Red Bull Cliff Diving World Cups.

Orlando Duque has established his home base in Hawaii because, apart from his girlfriend, water always has to be close by.

IMMORTAL:
The movie *9 Dives* documents the life of Orlando Duque and his highest jump so far, from a thirty-four-meter (112 ft) high bridge in Italy.

CHECK OUT:
www.9dives.com

10 X CLIFF DIVING WORLD CHAMPION

2009
Red Bull Cliff Diving World Series Champion

2010
2. place overall Red Bull Cliff Diving World Series

2012
2. place overall Red Bull Cliff Diving World Series

2013
High Diving world champion, FINA World Championship (Barcelona)

"The moment you are not afraid anymore practicing this sport is the moment you start living dangerously."

DO I REALLY HAVE TO EAT THIS NOW?!

[INTERVIEW]

WHEN DOES YOUR DISCIPLINED ATHLETE'S HEART BECOME WEAK? WHAT IS IT YOU NEVER PICK UP WITH A FORK?

ANYTHING sweet; I love it man. Crème brûlée in particular, or—something I learned to love in Austria—Kaiserschmarrn (sugared pancake with raisins). I really don't like fast food at all. Even if it is supposed to be fast, to me it is a waste of time.

WHAT WAS YOUR GREATEST FAUX PAS AS TO NUTRITION, EITHER BEFORE OR DURING A COMPETITION?

Back then I made the mistake of not eating anything at all. I was simply too excited and had to force myself to eat. Today I have a better routine of course, and I try to eat as well and as healthily as possible before competitions. But I am still excited before every dive.

WHO ARE THE THREE (LIVING OR HISTORIC) PERSONS SITTING NEXT TO YOU AT YOUR PERFECT DINNER?

My girlfriend Catalina, my mom, and my sister. They are the most important people in my life. Family is everything for me. More so as I am always traveling and can't see the people I love that often, so I want to make the time count that I can spend with these people.

WHAT CAN BE FOUND IN YOUR FREEZER?

Chicken or bacon for pasta carbonara, soy ice cream—and the bowl of the ice cream machine. I have no idea why it's in there (laughs).

THE TASTE OF YOUR CHILDHOOD IS ..

... oh, that depends. My mother went to the marketplace every morning and bought fresh food. I loved beans and soup, and salads always tasted great to me. And my father worked at a fruit distribution company, so we always had fresh fruit in our fridge. It was great!

WHAT WAS THE CRAZIEST THING YOU EVER ATE?

In the middle of China I was once offered a very special duck and they proudly presented it to me before cooking it. This duck had black feet and a black head. It was incredibly disturbing to see it lying there with bound feet, and I only thought: FUCK! Do I really have to eat this now?! It wasn't so bad after all, but I couldn't erase the image from my mind.

TRY TO COMPARE YOUR SPORT WITH A DISH. WHICH ONE COMES TO MIND?

It would have to be one where you know exactly what to do and how to do it. Where the preparation is actually more important than the cooking itself.

THE LONG WAY TO THE TOP

FAT BELLIES – FEW CALORIES.

The belly of fish yields particularly fine meat. "Because that's where the highest concentration of fat is located," says Roland Trettl, "and therefore the taste can develop more intensely." Nevertheless, fish is really quite low in calories, with the exception of tuna, which has more calories than the average pork cutlet.

HAWAIIAN STYLE POKE

15
MINUTES

SCALE
2

INGREDIENTS:

500 g (17½ oz) yellow mackerel filet
1 mango
1 onion
1 scallion
1 tsp fresh ginger
1 chili pod
2 tsp macadamia nuts
5 tsp soy sauce
3 tsp sesame oil
3 tsp sesame seeds
olive oil
lime zests
2 tsp chopped cilantro
sea salt

"Since I am here you have to show me everything."

Orlando Duque takes advantage of the short trip to Salzburg to cook his favorite meal with Roland Trettl to do some sightseeing.

During the evening he goes to the old part of town with his girlfriend: a stroll, romantic dinner, and so forth—no, Trettl doesn't have to be there, really (although he might, as a cook). But the master chef would be the perfect tour guide inside Hangar-7, he thinks.

So while Orlando, Catalina, and Roland walk through the building the topic of conversation switches from the exhibited vintage airplanes and the Formula 1 bodies to the inevitable topic whenever you are around Roland Trettl: food. In this case, Hawaiian food.

The executive chef is clearly fond of Orlando's favorite dish. Poke—pronounced "Poakay"—is a traditional Hawaiian cold appetizer. Roland himself got to know the dish a few years ago while on vacation.

"Poke is simple and quick to prepare, and it has this particular sour taste," he delights. "To top it off the dish is really wholesome.

"It's cool how many different variations you can cook with Poke. There's no limit to your imagination. Just take any fish you like and make it spicy-hot or fruity. Doesn't matter. As long as the ingredients are fresh."

Back in the kitchen Roland and Orlando get to work—as Roland stated previously, he's not very involved in this particular dish.

It's in the mix – Poke is so easy to prepare:

1. Cut the yellow fin mackerel into cube-sized pieces.

2. Cut mango into cubes.

3. Cut onion and scallion into slices.

4. Grate ginger.

5. Chop chili pod coarsely and macadamia nuts finely.

For the marinade, mix soy sauce, sesame oil, and sesame seeds. Trettl: "You can add a dash of olive oil if you like."

The dish is prepared inside a large bowl. Simply add all of the ingredients and stir thoroughly. Add lime zest and cilantro and season with salt.

A last tip:

While preparing the dish cool the bowl with ice. This way the fish keeps its perfect freshness up until the first bite.

"At home we don't have a chef. Sometimes I do the cooking, sometimes it is Catalina."

FREESTYLE SKIER

ITALY
RESIDENCE: LUTAGO

MARKUS EDER

BORN TO SKI.

NAME: Markus Eder

NICKNAME: Makke

BIRTHDAY: November 30, 1990

HEIGHT: 1.85 m (6')

WEIGHT: 85 kg (187 lbs)

DISCIPLINE: slopestyle, big air/slopestyle, back country freestyle

HOBBIES: climbing, trampolining, skating, slackline, biking, basketball

Just like many other kids from small mountain villages, Markus Eder learned how to ski right after learning how to walk. As opposed to others, he has almost forgotten how to walk since then, as he has spent more time on skis than on normal soles. To simply be fast wasn't enough for him from the very start. He wanted to express his creativity in the snow as well, and he found his holy grail the day he stood on freestyle skis for the first time. After that his career took shape. First he won a few regional competitions. Then came the national competitions.

His appearance on the international scene came at the Nine Knights Contest in 2010. Via a video contest he got a wildcard and was able to compete with the world's best freestyle skiers. A few hours later the rookie was standing on the podium—an almost magical story. Towards stellar success? The following months showed that his success was not fly-by-night. Although he lost one winter due to an injury, if you see him today with a broad smile doing his daring stunts you know this guy is motivated by the fun he is having. And because of that he can't be stopped.

"For our sport the Olympics are not that important. For example, the X-games or the Red Bull Playstreets are more important. Why? Because rules are not that essential in our discipline."

2011

1. place Polish Freeski Open
2. place Red Bull Linecatcher
1. place Mayrhofen Freeski Open
1. place SFR Tour France

2013

1. place Swatch Skiers Cup with Team Europe
1. place FWT Courmayeur

The path to ever more daring tricks is in small steps: at first the jumps get increasingly bigger. Later, rotation is added.

SOUTH-TYROLIAN AIRLINES.

[INTERVIEW]

WHO ARE THE THREE (LIVING OR HISTORIC) PERSONS SITTING AT THE TABLE OF YOUR PERFECT DINNER?

Rodney Mullen has an incredible, almost autistic personality, and this has made him the proverbial skate god. I would put the inventor of reggae Bob Marley on the list and Tyler the Creator, an American hip hop musician who is also a passionate skater.

WHICH FAMOUS SPORTSMAN/ SPORTSWOMAN WOULD YOU LIKE TO GO OUT TO DINNER WITH?

During summer I do a lot of climbing, so I would like to have dinner with Sasha de Guilian. She is currently the best climber in the world and is getting dangerously close to the top male climbers. And she is still pretty racy.

THE TASTE OF YOUR CHILDHOOD IS ...

... green Jell-O. We couldn't get it where we were living so friends always brought some over from Germany. It was just the greatest thing whenever it was around! But I haven't had it in at least fifteen years.

BEER IN THE GARDEN OR A GLASS OF WINE AT THE BAR?

I'll definitely take the beer; that's when it is almost certain we'll be goofing around with friends.

SWEET OR SOUR?

Sweet, all kinds of sweets.

WHAT WAS THE CRAZIEST THING YOU EVER ATE?

Veal tongue—that was pretty borderline. Let's change subject.

WHAT WAS IT YOU COULDN'T STAND AS A CHILD? AND DO YOU LIKE IT TODAY?

I have always eaten everything and anything ... no wait, I never liked Gröstl (grilled potatoes).

AT THE TABLE WITH FAMILY AND FRIENDS: ARE YOU THE FIRST ONE TO FINISH THEIR PLATE OR DO YOU ENJOY EVERY BITE?

Usually I am rather slow and enjoy the meal, but if it is really good I eat extremely fast.

WHAT CHARACTERISTIC UNITES A SUCCESSFUL FREESTYLE SKIER WITH A GOOD COOK?

Both depend on the subjective judgment of other people. Both live with the uncertainty whether people like it or not.

WHAT CAN BE FOUND IN YOUR FREEZER?

Home-made meat soup.

WHERE DOES THE FUN STOP WITH RESPECT TO FOOD?

With soft-boiled noodles. And with almost all the noodles I eat outside of Italy. Eighty percent of it is really bad. Pasta is one of the few things I know how to cook, so I know a little about it.

COOKING IS ...

... a nice pastime, now and then. I have to admit I'm not that good at it.

THE LONG WAY TO THE TOP

DUMPLING-SECRETS.

There are few dishes with as many half-truths and wrong home recipes as dumplings. For example, many believe that more eggs are good for dumplings. The opposite is true. The more eggs, the more firm the consistency of the dumplings. Or rolling the dumplings: many put flour on their palms, but it works better if you moisten your hands with water. In case the dumpling dough doesn't bind well and the dumplings keep falling apart, adding a bit of flour helps.

SOUTH TYROLIAN SPINACH-CHEESE GNOCCHI

WITH BACON COLESLAW

40 MINUTES

SCALE 5

INGREDIENTS:
250 g (9 oz) buns from yesterday
80 g (2¾ oz) milk
1/2 onion
300 g (10½ oz) leaf spinach
1 garlic clove
oil
80 g (2¾ oz) scamorza
chives
flour
2 eggs
parmesan cheese
80 g (2¾ oz) butter
1 dash of pepper
1 dash of nutmeg

BACON COLESLAW:
1/2 onion
40 g (1½ oz) pork belly
60 g (2 oz) olive oil
60 g (2 oz) white wine vinegar
salt and pepper
300 g (10½ oz) white cabbage

A South Tyrolian who can cook but doesn't ski meets a South Tyrolian who can ski but can't cook. A bad mix? Not in the kitchen of Ikarus. And least of all if it is about a South Tyrolian national dish.

"You have been in Salzburg for ten years? Crazy." Roland Trettl couldn't have gotten more incomprehension, regardless of all the success, regardless of the fact that during this time the Ikarus has grown into an international player on the culinary scene. "I won't allow them to get me out of South Tirol," Eder adds. Trettl's intent on explaining why he left his home sounds almost like an apology. The Salzburg airport, the many trips to the guest cooks of Ikarus, the faraway location of South Tirol. They quickly agree to bring a piece of home into the kitchen and start cooking.

Part 1 of the choreography: BACON COLESLAW

Markus starts chopping the onion and the bacon into small cubes to prepare the marinade for the coleslaw. Then he braises the onion in olive oil and adds bacon after a few minutes. Once the bacon is nice and crispy Eder adds white wine vinegar and seasons with salt and pepper.

Meanwhile, Trettl has chopped the white cabbage into thin slices about 1/2 cm (¼") wide and 7 cm (2¾") long. The warm marinade is now poured over the cabbage—this way it will get absorbed better—and everything is left to rest for half an hour.

Part 2: SPINACH-CHEESE GNOCCHI.

Buns from the day before get a new delicious destination with this recipe: Trettl cuts them into thin slices and soaks them in milk.

Meanwhile, Eder chops up the onion and cleans and cuts the leaf spinach and the garlic cloves. All of it is braised in hot oil in a pan until the spinach collapses. Eder allows the spinach to cool down and drains the contents of the pan through a sieve.

All the while Trettl prepares the remaining ingredients for the gnocchi dough: he grates the scamorza with a coarse grater into longish strips and chops up chives. Then he mixes the soaked white bread with the cheese and sprinkles some flour over it. The eggs are broken over the mix and he adds the chives and a dash of milk and seasons with nutmeg and pepper. Markus is kneading spinach and onion into the gnocchi dough.

The two chefs roll the dough into longish gnocchi and place it into gently simmering water for ten minutes. At the same time Trettl grates the parmesan and heats the butter in a pan until it is golden. Eder picks up the gnocchi with a skimmer, allows them to drip off well, and then puts them into deep plates. He then adds the Parmesan and the molten butter over the gnocchi. After the first bite Eder shakes his head.

The finish: HOME FOR THE PALATE.

"I was in New Zealand for two months with a trained cook. Why didn't he know how to do it?" Most probably because he would have to prepare the dish every night to cure homesickness.

"This guy hasn't had enough gnocchi! I always heard this saying from my dad whenever I was too weak to do anything. Gnocchi are the traditional Red Bull for South Tyrolians."

RACE CAR DRIVER

SWEDEN
RESIDENCE: SALENSTEIN, SWITZERLAND

MATTIAS EKSTRÖM

THE LORD OF THE RINGS.

NAME: Mattias Ekström

BIRTHDAY: July 14, 1978

HEIGHT: 1.83 m (6')

WEIGHT: 79 kg (174 lbs)

DISCIPLINE: DTM

HOBBIES: rallycross, quad, tennis, and his dogs

WEBSITE: www.mattiasekstrom.com

FACEBOOK: www.facebook.com/mattiasekstrom.racing

Is speed inheritable? In the case of a few athletes the probability seems quite high. Mattias Ekström is such an example. During the 1990s his father Bengt was a successful rallycross pilot. In 1993, his son started his racing career in carting. Today, Mattias Ekström is among the most versatile racing pilots of our time.

Whether asphalt, gravel, or hall floors, the Audi pilot is fast on any surface, so he looks forward to challenges not only at the DTM (Deutsche Tourenwagen Meisterschaft - German Touring Car Championship), but also in rally racing, long-distance races and, very successfully, at the "Race of Champions," which he won several times. In 2010, the Swede discovered a passion for NASCAR after successful tests in the US. However, his focus is still on the DTM, which he joined as early as 2001, and since then he has maintained his loyalty to Team ABT. In 2004 and 2007 he won the series.

Proverbial motor sports legend Walter Röhrl thinks Mattias Ekström is currently one of the most complete touring car pilots.

DTM

Overall victory 2004 and 2007, over fifty spots on the podium in twelve years

RALLY

Overall winner group N, Rally Sweden and Rally Catalonia 2004

RACE OF CHAMPIONS

Winner 2006 (Paris), 2007 (Wembley), and 2009 (Beijing)

NATIONS CUP

Winner 2005 (Paris)

The sequence before the race is always similar for Mattias: he eats two hours before the competition. Then there is a short nap of fifteen to thirty minutes.

THE SWEDISH EXPRESS.

[INTERVIEW]

WHICH TWO (STILL LIVING OR HISTORIC) PERSONS ARE SITTING AT THE TABLE OF YOUR PERFECT DINNER?

Juan Pablo Montoya, because he is a really fun guy, and Travis Pastrana. I don't know him personally and he probably doesn't have any food culture, but that's perhaps the reason why it would be quite exciting.

WHICH FAMOUS SPORTSMAN/ SPORTSWOMAN WOULD YOU LIKE TO GO OUT TO DINNER WITH?

With Aksel Lund Svindal, because he is a very entertaining fellow.

WHAT WAS THE CRAZIEST THING YOU EVER ATE?

That's still ahead. Regarding food I am very conservative and careful.

WHAT WAS IT YOU COULDN'T STAND AS A CHILD? AND DO YOU LIKE IT TODAY?

I hated fish with egg sauce. I couldn't stand the eggs. Today a good egg is downright fun.

AT THE TABLE WITH FAMILY AND FRIENDS: ARE YOU THE FIRST ONE TO FINISH YOUR PLATE OR DO YOU ENJOY EVERY BITE?

Unfortunately I am always the first. I eat way too quickly. But I can eat more than anyone else.

YOU ARE PLANNING A ROMANTIC DINNER FOR TWO: WHERE DOES IT TAKE PLACE?

In Sweden. During summer. With its long and luminous evenings you can take your time with dinners.

WHICH CHARACTERISTIC UNITES A SUCCESSFUL DTM PILOT WITH A GOOD COOK?

The details! And a preoccupation with the quality of the ingredients.

YOU WAKE UP IN THE MIDDLE OF THE NIGHT WITH THE MUNCHIES. WHAT HAS TO BE IN YOUR FRIDGE?

Lactose-free low-fat cheese. A glass of milk. And crispbread, of course.

WHAT CAN BE FOUND IN YOUR FREEZER?

Ice cream for my young son and ground beef for the dogs (smirking). Okay, the ice cream is for me too ...

WHERE DOES THE FUN STOP REGARDING FOOD?

With bad noodles, overcooked vegetables, and meat that spent too much time in the pan.

COOKING IS ...

... relaxing. If you are not good at something you have to make an effort and have no time to think about something else. That's how I relax.

THE LONG WAY TO THE TOP

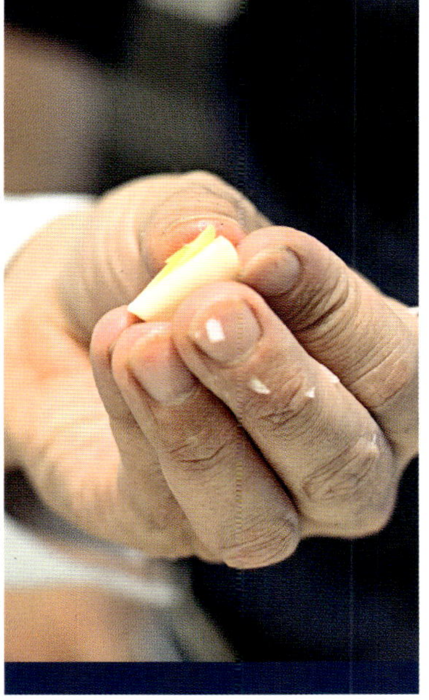

GARLIC – THE ROOT OF EVIL.

As good as garlic tastes, many avoid it to escape well-known evaporations or because even small amounts can cause bothersome burping. Both of these symptoms of this healthy plant can be significantly diminished by removing the germ of each clove before processing. Another tip for achieving a better taste: instead of grinding up the aromatic compounds in a garlic press it is better to finely chop the cloves.

FUSILLI BOLOGNESE

À LA EKSTRÖM

30 MINUTES

SCALE **3**

INGREDIENTS:
1 onion
10 cherry tomatoes
150 g (5 oz) champignons
1 zucchini
50 g (1¾ oz) olive oil
150 g (5 oz) ground pork
150 g (5 oz) ground beef
salt
1 sprig of thyme
1 tsp chili powder
600 g (21 oz) fusilli
basil leaves
60 g (2 oz) milk
grana padano (as desired)

What can you do wrong with noodles? Don't ever ask this question in the presence of Mattias Ekström or Roland Trettl.

You would most certainly receive a lecture of several minutes. And your reputation would immediately crash to the level of a student driver who has failed the test five times in a row. The theoretical test, that is.

But let's get back to the start. Roland Trettl stands in front of the ingredients and looks expectantly at Mattias Ekström. "How long does a bolognese take in your case?" "Forty minutes. Including eating, that is. Sometimes less," he adds with a laugh when he sees Trettl's dumbfounded expression:

"I am a sportsman, not a cook."

Right now, worlds are colliding in front of the stainless steel stove of Ikarus. Should a reader ever enjoy a bolognese à la Trettl, time should not be much of an issue. Three hours should be expected at the very least, according to the chef. "Now I understand the addition à la Ekström: because it has to be fast."

To not lose any more time both of them get to work preparing the ingredients. They chop the onion, quarter the cherry tomatoes, and cut up the champignons. Before Trettl chops up the zucchini he removes the white pulp. "It has so little taste that I only use the generously carved-out skin."

Meanwhile, a pot with heated olive oil is waiting on the stove. First, the executive chef of Ikarus adds the onions into the pot and braises them until they are golden-yellow. From the second starting position the ground meat enters the race of the best Bolognese— and Roland Trettl at first looks the other way. "It's burning!" warns Ekström with a slightly alarmed voice concerning the carelessness of the chef. "It's supposed to, the roasted ingredients provide the unique flavor to the bolognese. That's why I don't work with teflon pans," the cook replies and starts to scrape the roasted ground meat from the bottom of the pan with much effort. Again and again he allows the meat to slightly burn before stirring it. Only now does he add salt to the meat and also answers the question why: because otherwise it would soak up water. Once the meat is well cooked Trettl prepares the champignons, then the zucchini and, keeping some distance, the cherry tomatoes, and adds them to the Bolognese. By now he needs both his hands to stir the ingredients.

When Trettl takes notice of Ekström's smirking expression he says dryly, "This is the sport of a cook." After seasoning the Bolognese with finely chopped thyme and some chili-paprika powder, both cooks contemplate their creation. "The colors are great, my kids would love this dish right away," the racecar driver remarks with satisfaction.

The engine of the Bolognese is now pretty much ready and the sauce continues to simmer at medium temperature. Let's get to the chassis now—cooking the pasta. Ekström turns out to be a real connoisseur of the matter, and he recounts traumatic events as a child involving soft-boiled pasta, the habit of some team cooks to serve the noodles way too hard, and the challenge to find the best moment to take the pasta out of the water.

He has never found a more receptive listener of his descriptions. Trettl does away with folk wisdom, housewife tales, and other pasta lies, summing up in the following seven pasta commandments:

"My son would love this dish right away, just because of the colors. They are great."

THE SEVEN PASTA COMMANDMENTS.

1. YOU SHALL ADD ENOUGH SALT TO THE WATER FOR THE PASTA!

And not just a pinch of salt, but sufficient so that the water is nicely over-salted. Roland throws three handful of salt into the pot. Only then will the salt be absorbed by the pasta. Adding salt before eating doesn't allow for an even and subtle taste.

2. YOU SHALL USE ENOUGH WATER!

Per 100 g (3½ oz) of pasta, 1 liter (¼ gal) of water is perfect. It is best to always use oversized pots.

3. YOU SHALL TRUST NO "AL DENTE" DEFINITION, BECAUSE THERE IS NONE!

The famous "bite" of pasta is a matter of interpretation. South Italians like their pasta significantly harder than South Tyrolians like Roland Trettl. His trick: he always takes the noodles from the water when they are still too hard and then adds the sauce, allowing the pasta to reach the perfect state.

4. YOU SHALL NOT RINSE THE PASTA WITH COLD WATER!

Most likely the most widely-practiced deadly sin among pasta cooks. Pasta loses its starch when it is rinsed.

5. YOU SHALL NOT ADD OIL TO THE NOODLE WATER!

Popular misconception number two: oil helps noodles not stick together. This may well be so, but more than anything it causes the pores of the pasta to gum up, preventing them from soaking up taste and sauce.

6. YOU SHALL USE WHITE PASTA!

Whole grain and other noodles are certainly justified, but when it's about finding the perfect match for a grand sauce there is no way around pasta made from hard wheat.

7. YOU SHALL USE THE RIGHT PASTA FOR YOUR SAUCE!

Varying shapes of noodles have their reason: they are supposed to soak up the corresponding sauce as well as possible. Fusilli are a good general choice; due to their "thread" they soak up really well.

Just before the pasta is taken out of the water Roland Trettl performs the last operations with the Bolognese. He adds milk, as well as a few finely chopped basil leaves. They should only be added at the very end, as the essential oils react very sensitively. Now there's grated cheese, olive oil, and a good dash of ground white pepper being added. Then Trettl stirs the pasta in the pot with the Bolognese.

"The good thing about Bolognese is that I can adjust it to my training. When I do more physical workout I add more meat. When endurance is primary I increase the amount of noodles."

"Do you know why I started to cook for myself?," asks Ekström after testing the joint creation. "Because I wanted to eat something I like. Good food makes for a good mood. And this one here makes a really good mood. Real fusilli à la Ekström, tuned by Roland. Unfortunately, I don't always have the fresh herbs handy in my RV; they provide this special freshness."

This opinion by the way was shared unanimously by the professionals of the Ikarus: among the best pasta they had ever tasted. No surprise considering these two pasta experts.

There are very few other things where Ekström can relax as much as with cooking. For this reason he usually cooks for himself in his RV before races.

PROFESSIONAL MOUNTAINEER
AND EXTREME CLIMBER

GERMANY
RESIDENCE: BERG AT LAKE STARNBERG

STEFAN GLOWACZ

IT TAKES DISTANCE TO PROVIDE CLOSENESS.

NAME: Stefan Glowacz

BIRTHDAY: March 22, 1965

HEIGHT: 1.80 m (5' 9")

WEIGHT: 65 kg (143 lbs)

DISCIPLINE: free climbing

HOBBIES: kiting, road racing, city tours

WEBSITE: www.glowacz.de

Stefan Glowacz is Germany's most well-known free climber and a father of three. His personal conviction allows him to live both with one hundred percent commitment. It is the certainty that there is only one way for him. It leads the forty-eight-year-old to unknown locations and onto unconquered mountaintops. But it also brings him back home.

Only the combination of faraway adventures and the safety of the family makes him a complete and happy person. Hence, he says, an attentive and caring father and husband. A man whose closeness you can only experience when you let him go.

Early schooling: "When I was a child I used to climb onto any rock while my family was trekking."

2004

First ascent Titlis, Engelberg/ Switzerland "Letzte Ausfahrt Titlis" ("Last Exit Titlis") (X-)

2006

Climbing expedition to the Acopan tepui table mountain in Venezuela, first ascent of the "Purgatory" route (IX)

2008

Climbing expedition to Baffin Island, ascent of the "The Bastions" route (X-) at the "Buchan Gulf"

2009

Climbing expedition Minas Gerais/ Brazil "Place of Happiness" (IX); nonstop intent of the "Royal Flash" route at the Fitz Roy/Patagonia

2010

First ascent of the "Behind the Rainbow" route (IX+/X-) at the Roraima table mountain in the border triangle between British Guyana, Venezuela, and Brazil.

2013

The Red Bull 7 Giants was a series of extraordinary first ascents in the Republic of Komi, Russia.

Hunter of the Moment: The film documents the spectacular tour of Stefan Glowacz from the deepest Venezuelan jungle up to the 2,723 meter (8,933 ft) Roraima rock.

CHOCOLATE AND FISH EMBRYOS.

[INTERVIEW]

THE TASTE OF YOUR CHILDHOOD IS ...

... definitely cheesecake. My mother used to make a cake every Friday, usually cheesecake. It has followed me through my entire childhood. I still love it, particularly the American version, the soft and fat one.

WHAT IS IT YOU COULDN'T STAND AS A CHILD? AND DO YOU LIKE IT TODAY?

Russian eggs and sprouts. Especially sprouts. If there were any sprouts in a dish I went ballistic (laughs). With time this has changed, fortunately. Today it is okay, but it is still not my favorite dish.

WHICH CHARACTERISTIC UNITES A SUCCESSFUL SPORTSMAN WITH A GOOD COOK?

Definitely the passion for what you do. This applies across the professions. As a cook you need a certain sensitivity to be perfect at your craft. This is not much different from many climbers. I am a very sensitive and sensual person; I love the haptik, the feel of sculptures and rock types, or the sight of certain rock formations. Once you have found your passion you develop a sort of instinct that you can not explain. Simply because for you it is obvious and natural, whether as a climber or a cook. It's in your guts.

WHAT WAS THE CRAZIEST THING YOU EVER ATE?

On my tours I visit many countries where it is customary to serve the guest a traditional dish. The craziest thing must have been some kind of fish embryo in Japan—that was a tough one which didn't go beyond tasting it. And raw whale from Greenland is not exactly a culinary highlight. You chew forever on these rubbery things and think: "Oh God, please let this be over soon!"

THE FRIDGE OF A PERSON SAYS A LOT ABOUT HIS CHARACTER. WHAT DOES IT LOOK LIKE IN YOUR CASE?

These days my fridge is pretty much empty, because at home food has to be spontaneous and fresh. The family meeting is in the morning; I go and do the shopping and during the evening we all cook together. Ever since we have been doing it this way my kids have gotten an entirely different relationship to food. I think it is simply great that my son wants to go to dinner at the Tantris to celebrate his diploma (Note: a 2-star restaurant in Munich).

WHAT ARE YOUR CRITERIA TO PUT TOGETHER YOUR PROVISIONS FOR A LONG TOUR?

On tour the main thing is energy provision and saving on weight—taste plays no role, really. I eat mostly dried food where you add hot water and energy bars. And some chocolate, to give yourself a treat.

YOU ARE FAR AWAY FROM ANY CIVILIZATION AND HAVE BEEN GOING FOR A LONG TIME. WHAT DISH ARE YOU THINKING ABOUT?

Often it's just a piece of chocolate. With raisins and nuts is best, then I am totally happy. That's just simply a dream come true. I don't need anything else.

THE LONG WAY TO THE TOP

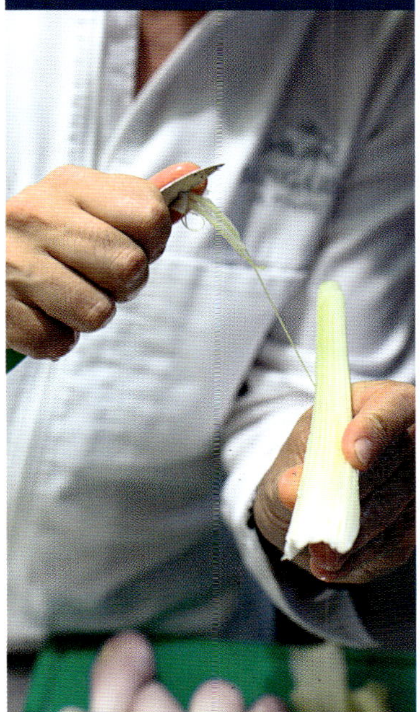

CELERY: TASTE IN EVERY FIBER.

It is best to use a knife to peel and clean celery. Wash the celery, cut off both ends, and remove the hard fibers with a potato peeler. These hard fibers are great for stews, while the stem of the celery goes with the vegetables.

VEAL CHEEKS

WITH ROCKET SALAD POLENTA AND OVEN VEGETABLES

150
MINUTES

SCALE
7

INGREDIENTS:
8 veal cheeks
salt, pepper
2 celery stalks
1 onion
2 carrots
1 TBSP tomato paste
150 g (5 oz) white wine
1 garlic clove
1 laurel leaf
300 g (10 oz) veal stock
(or water)
100 g (3½) potatoes

ROCKET SALAD POLENTA:
400 g (13½ oz) poultry stock
or water
1 sprig of thyme
1 garlic clove
2 bunch of rocket lettuce
200 g (7 oz) polenta
50 g (1¾ oz) olive oil

OVEN VEGETABLES:
4 celery stalks
1 red onion
4 carrots
30 g (1 oz) butter
20 g (¾ oz) olive oil

"I don't like repetition because I know the second time won't be as good as the first time," says Stefan Glowacz. It is precisely this attitude that drives him to constant new challenges on his tours. And in the case of cooking, the top athlete is faithful to his motto and faces a new challenge with his favorite dish, because braised veal cheeks with rocket salad polenta are a first ascent for him. Fortunately, with Roland Trettl he has a professional at his side.

"Cooking has its very own kind of aesthetic—just like climbing."

The fact that Trettl and Glowacz immediately hit it off is not only due to Glowacz's great interest in cooking, but also because of a friend they have in common: Austria's top chef Hans Haas. Trettl's former employer's cookbook is the place where this recipe for veal cheeks came from—a rather special challenge for Trettl to add his very own personal note to the dish. After a lively discussion concerning the use of ice in combination with meat the two pros get to work, cutting the veal cheeks to size and seasoning them with salt and pepper. Trettl suggests to Glowacz to trust your feeling both when buying and cooking meat while Glowacz peels the celery with the potato peeler.

After the vegetables have been chopped the calf cheeks are braised for two minutes on each side. While the meat is still cooking, coarsely chopped onion, celery, and carrots are added. Countless questions by Glowacz prove that his hunger for knowledge is at par with his real hunger.

Now the calf cheeks are briefly removed from the pot to braise the vegetables. After adding tomato paste the vegetables are deglazed with white wine and garlic, salt, and a laurel leaf are added. The vegetables serve as a taste carrier and provide color to the dish. For this reason Trettl always suggests removing the sediment from the pot to get an intense aroma. After the wine has almost entirely evaporated the meat is put back into the pot, veal stock is added and seasoned, and then left to stew in the oven for about two hours at low heat after adding chopped potatoes.

While the meat simmers there is sufficient time to take care of the polenta. Trettl uses poultry stock, olive oil, thyme, and garlic. Glowacz is surprised at the speed with which the ingredients are handed to Trettl and jokes:

"I would love to have these kinds of helpers at home in the kitchen!"

For the polenta, Trettl suggests a rather narrow pot with a good height. Cook the polenta in the stock until there is a thick burnt layer at the bottom. "Even many professionals do this the wrong way," says Trettl, "because the burnt part of polenta is the best!" To keep the yellow color of the polenta he chops the rocket salad and folds it in.

The one thing still missing is the oven vegetables, but they don't take much time. You only have to chop up the vegetables and heat the olive oil and the butter until they are light brown. Add 100 g (3½ oz) of water and 2 TBSP of the veal cheek sauce and allow to simmer for about ten minutes while covered until the vegetables are nice and soft.

When Glowacz takes out the veal cheeks after two hours Trettl is visibly excited by the result. "Meat and sauce of braised dishes always have to form a unit," he explains to Glowacz while he

tastes the sauce. And Trettl's last words before eating show that although there are two pros at work, they are first and foremost men:

"Look at this sauce, the binding and the shine. This is Champion's League."

SOCCER PLAYER

GERMANY
RESIDENCE: FLORENCE, ITALY

MARIO GÓMEZ

THE TORERO.

NAME: Mario Gómez

BIRTHDAY: July 10, 1985

HEIGHT: 1.89 m (6' 2")

WEIGHT: 88 kg (194 lbs)

POSITION: striker

NUMBER: 33

HOBBIES: meet friends, music, tennis

WEBSITE: www.mario-gomez.de

Until recently he was the most expensive transfer within the German Bundesliga. He became the leading goalscorer in Germany, played three finals in the Champions League, has been a member of the national team for years, and has always demonstrated his qualities at important matches. All of this sounds like a storybook career, with only the sunny sides of pro soccer. However, as simple as it sounds, it hasn't always been like that for Gómez. With the burden of a transfer fee of 35 million Euros (50,050,000 US) in 2009, he switched from the VfB Stuttgart to Bayern Munich, where he met a trainer who did not count on him. Gómez' answer was goals. Many goals: forty-four of them under this very same trainer. And a place in the national soccer team.

After defeats in semifinals and finals with the German National Team a "vice-champion season" followed with Bayern Munich—something of a catastrophe for the club, spoiled by success. The lost Champions League Final at the home stadium was particularly discouraging. Quickly there was talk about the generation that can't win. Thanks to Mario Gómez' ability to bounce back—among other factors—the next year turned out to be a record season. As the first German team they won the triple crown, including the Champions League. Despite the fact that his contract ran for three more years, Gómez left Bayern Munich and fulfilled his teenage dream: he switched to the south, to Italy's AC Florence. After years of dominance, Milano and Juventus are to be kicked off the throne. Not an easy undertaking and certainly not an easy path, but they have the right guy as a striker.

CHAMPIONS LEAGUE WINNER 2013

2 x Champions League Finalist (2010, 2012)

3 x GERMAN CHAMPION

2007, 2010, 2013

2 x DFB TROPHY

2010, 2013

GERMANY'S SOCCER PLAYER 2007

BUNDESLIGA LEADING GOALSCORER 2010/11

WORLD CHAMPIONSHIP: THIRD IN 2010

EUROPEAN CHAMPIONSHIP: FINALIST IN 2008; SEMIFINALIST IN 2012

Gómez makes history: he wins the triple crown with the Bavarians. FC Bayern is the first German team that succeeds at winning the Champions League, the German Championship, and the DFB Trophy in one season. After hiring Gómez, Florence is dreaming about the future as well!

COMEBACK KID. ALSO WITH FOOD.

[INTERVIEW]

WHICH LIVING OR HISTORIC PERSON IS SITTING AT THE TABLE OF YOUR PERFECT DINNER?

Banksy! Nobody knows him, nobody knows what he looks like—now that would be a real surprise for a change.

WHICH FAMOUS SPORTSMAN WOULD YOU LIKE TO HAVE DINNER WITH?

With Romario; he was the idol of my childhood. During the World Championship of 1994 we were on vacation in South Tirol. And then Italy of all nations gets into the final against Brazil, and I was pretty much the only one on Brazil's side because of Romario.

THE TASTE OF YOUR CHILDHOOD IS ...

... rice soufflé with vanilla sauce!

BEER IN THE GARDEN OR A GLASS OF WINE AT THE BAR?

Both. During my time in Munich I learned to like beer gardens quite a lot, but I also like a decent glass of wine in a nice atmosphere.

WHAT WAS THE CRAZIEST THING YOU EVER ATE?

On principle I don't eat anything crazy. That's also because I have a shellfish allergy. It came from one day to the next, and I went through much pain to learn what happens when you can't stomach something.

AT THE TABLE WITH FAMILY AND FRIENDS: ARE YOU THE FIRST ONE TO FINISH OR DO YOU ENJOY EVERY BITE?

I am definitely a fast eater (while he puts his empty plate aside Roland Trettl hasn't even made it halfway through his portion).

WHICH CHARACTERISTIC UNITES A SUCCESSFUL SOCCER PLAYER WITH A GOOD COOK?

Discipline and fun.

WHERE DOES THE FUN STOP REGARDING FOOD?

With shellfish. And very quickly at that. After years of abstinence I tried prawns again, and in no time I was running to the toilet to throw up. Not a chance. Sorry.

TRY TO COMPARE YOUR SPORT WITH A DISH. WHICH ONE COMES TO MIND?

Pizza, because everyone loves it! It is colorful and cheerful, and great fun.

COOKING IS ...

... compensation—and good times with friends.

THE LONG WAY TO THE TOP

TATAR – ONLY BARBARIANS USE THE MEAT GRINDER.

The name tatar goes back to the Tartars, who are rumored to have placed raw pieces of meat under their saddles to ride them tender before consuming them. Did the Turks from Middle-Age Eurasia have a meat grinder? Certainly not. Today, a meat grinder has no business in the preparation of some good tatar, as a large part of its aroma gets lost when grinding the meat.

FINISH IN FLORENCE.

We almost had to do without the cooking skills of currently perhaps the best German striker. At least for this book. Although the date with Mario had already been set up in April 2013, it never got to that. The culprit was the goal instinct of the son of a German mother and a Spanish father: his goal for the 2:0 during the semifinal home game of the Champions League against Barcelona and his hat trick within six minutes during the DFB Trophy semifinal against VfL Wolfsburg made it possible for Bayern Munich to advance in all competitions—and Gómez had no time for cooking. With two goals in the final and the historic triple Mario said goodbye at the end of the season as one of the most successful strikers in the long history of the club in Munich and went to Florence. After moving, and the preparation for the season, there happened to be a short time window for a visit by the goal-getter, who was greeted frenetically.

BISON TATAR

WITH POTATO-RÖSTI

30 MINUTES

SCALE 5

RÖSTI:
400 g (14 oz) potatoes
1 TBSP olive oil
20 g (¾ oz) butter
salt, pepper

TATAR:
400 g (14 oz) bison filet
1 shallot
2 egg yolk
1 TBSP soy sauce
1 TBSP mustard
1 TBSP cognac
lime juice
1 dash of chi i powder
2 TBSP fried onions
1 handful of rocket lettuce
1 garlic clove
3 TBSP olive oil
sea salt

Sous-chef of the Four Seasons Roberto Cessherini assisted Trettl and Gómez with his amazingly affectionate hospitality in his kitchen, but the bison filet—which traveled in the on-board luggage—also piqued his interest.

This time the athlete was not asked about his preferred dish. Roland Trettl—as an Italian obviously a "Tifoso"—had already made the choice. "I read that every time Mario had eaten bison meat he struck a goal. So we are taking care of the perfect start of the season for this guy!"

On his flight to Florence, Trettl not only took along his knives, spices, and apron but had a perfect piece of American bison meat in his luggage. Perfectly packed inside an ice box, of course.

As Gómez had not yet moved into a new apartment after his transfer there was no kitchen available. Vito Mollica—a cook and friend of Trettl and the chef of the Four Seasons Hotel in Florence—immediately agreed to provide a section of his hotel kitchen.

Two days before AC Florence would kick off the season with a qualifying match for the European League against GC Zurich, the moment had finally arrived. Mario Gómez was standing in the kitchen next to Roland Trettl, who handed him the potato peeler without much ado. Mario went to work. "Great, another athlete with a talent for cooking!," Trettl comments while the first peels fall down. After Gómez has also finely grated the potatoes, Trettl takes over. He seasons the mix with salt and pepper and then squeezes out the liquid with his hands. This is now evenly distributed inside the pan that Trettl previously rubbed with olive oil, until finally there is a flat cake about 2 cm (¾") thick. He uses a fork to firmly press it into the bottom of the pan. The rösti remain in the pan until they are brown. Trettl adds butter only later so they don't burn early on.

Raw meat.

Gómez had acknowledged the bison recipe with a gleam in his eyes. "I wasn't prepared for bison, rather, some spätzle or pizza. So much the better, bison has always brought me luck." So now number 33, with Trettl's razor-sharp knives in hand, awaits his orders, as we don't want any fingertips to "season" the meat.

Gómez starts to cut up the bison filet into fine cubes and puts it in a bowl. He peels, cuts, and chops the shallot into cubes and adds it to the bison. Now follow the remaining ingredients: 2 egg yolks, soy sauce, mustard, cognac, juice of ½ a lime, 1 TBSP olive oil, 1 dash of salt, the chili powder, the finely chopped garlic, and the roasted onions go into the bowl and are thoroughly mixed with

the meat. With a spoon the tatar is shaped into gnocchi and seasoned with sea salt and ground pepper. Rocket lettuce leaves with their spicy aroma round off the taste.

While eating, a smirk crosses the face of Gómez.

"The taste of the meat is more delicate, more elegant than beef. Beef tastes more 'meaty.' Every day I discover something new here. When I explore the city I find a new area that I like even better than the one the day before almost every day. And now a new dish, too."

By the way, the away game against the Zurich Grasshoppers two days later was won 2:1. The second goal was ruled an own goal as a defensive player had touched the strike to the goal with a slide tackle. Mario Gómez was the shooter ...

The stuff from which dreams are made of: some 265 million people worldwide play soccer. If they were to pick up Mario's secret recipe for scoring goals, bison would soon become extinct.

SAILORS

AUSTRIA
RESIDENCE: WINDEN AM SEE (HAGARA)
BZW. ZELL AM SEE (STEINACHER)

ROMAN HAGARA & HANS-PETER STEINACHER

AGAINST ALL RULES.

NAME: Roman Hagara

BIRTHDAY: April 30, 1966

HEIGHT: 1.71 m (5' 6")

WEIGHT: 68 kg (150 lbs)

PROFESSION: carpenter, licensed sailing instructor

DISCIPLINE: Sailing Extreme Series

HOBBIES: photography, mountain biking, carpentry, nature

WEBSITE: www.redbullextremesailing.com

NAME: Hans-Peter Steinacher

BIRTHDAY: September 9, 1968

HEIGHT: 1.80 m (5' 9")

WEIGHT: 73 kg (161 lbs)

PROFESSION: regular soldier

DISCIPLINE: Sailing Extreme Series

HOBBIES: ice hockey, tennis

WEBSITE: www.redbullextremesailing.com

Summer sports in Austria? And of all things, sailing?! Not many parents in the land of mountains and ski gods would advise their children in this regard. Fortunately, in the case of Roman Hagara and Hans-Peter Steinacher, it was not any different. The Tornado sailors became Austria's most successful summer sports athletes of all time. Two Olympic gold medals in Sydney and Athens are the absolute highlights of a career that is now almost three decades old. And they are not through yet, proving it with their top results at the Extreme Sailing Series and, away from their own catamaran, as instructors for the America's Youth Cup. "You can sail even if you are of advanced age" the two say with a suggestive grin. So firm land will have to wait for now.

Unity makes them strong: Roman is the helmsman while Hans-Peter takes care of tactics.

2 X AUSTRIAN SPORTSMAN OF THE YEAR (2000/2004)

2000
Olympic champion (Sydney)
European champion (Allasio)

2001
European champion (St. Moritz)

2004
Olympic champion (Athens)

2006
European champion (Travemünde)

2012
Extreme Sailing Series '12:
2 x 2. place
1 x 3. place

High speed and adrenaline: the Extreme Sailing Series brings action back into sailing.

WITH KAISER-SCHMARREN TO A BEHEMOTH.

[INTERVIEW]

WHAT MAKES YOUR DISCIPLINED ATHLETE HEARTS WEAK? WHAT WOULD YOU NEVER PICK UP WITH A FORK?

Steinacher: I can do without everything except for beer.

Hagara: My heart always gets weak with a Kaiserschmarren (sugared pancake with raisins). And I don't eat tuna—not because I don't like it, but because it is an endangered species due to overfishing. It's not really necessary.

WHAT WAS YOUR GREATEST MISTAKE AS TO NUTRITION BEFORE OR DURING A COMPETITION?

Hagara: It happened not too long ago, a sandwich with rancid mayonnaise. It turned my stomach upside down.

Steinacher: Shili is not a good idea either; we don't have a toilet while on the water (laughs).

WHAT DOES THE EVENING AND THE MORNING BEFORE A COMPETITION LOOK LIKE IN YOUR CASE? WHAT'S ON YOUR PLATES AND IN YOUR GLASSES?

Hagara: In the evening we eat all we can. In the morning we have something light, such as granola, yogurt, and fruit.

HOW DO YOU CELEBRATE A SUCCESSFUL COMPETITION?

Hagara: As a complete teetotaler, with water only.

Steinacher: And I' l have a beer with the crew.

LET'S SAY YOU GET A DATE WITH LINDSEY VONN FOR DINNER. WHERE WOULD YOU TAKE HER?

Steinacher: Up to the alps, there's no sin there (laughs).

Hagara: Lindsey? I prefer to pamper my wife with my own cooking skills.

YOU HAVE ONE LAST MEAL. WHAT WOULD YOU ORDER?

Steinacher: Stuffed peppers.

Hagara: Kaiserschmarren until the cows come home.

A LOOK INTO THE CRYSTAL BALL: WHAT COMES AFTER YOUR CAREER—MORE SIXPACK ABS OR SIX PACK WITH BACON WRAP?

Hagara: I will look like Georg Fundack, our Olympic team coach: a 130-kilo (286 lb) behemoth (laughs).

Steinacher: And I'll stay healthy.

THE LONG WAY TO THE TOP

BEAUTY QUEEN CARROT.

Carrots are veritable vitamin bombs, mostly due to their perfect skin. If you boil carrots you should therefore only rasp them lightly and not peel them completely.

BEET SOUP

WITH HORSERADISH CREAM

20 MINUTES

SCALE 1

INGREDIENTS:

- 400 g (14 oz) beets
- 90 g (3 oz) shallots
- olive oil
- 600 g (21 oz) vegetable stock
- 3 TBSP balsamic vinegar
- salt
- pepper
- 120 g (4¼ oz) sour cream
- 50 g (1¾ oz) creamy horseradish
- 4 tsp fresh horseradish
- 4 tsp fresh chives

A day by the sea ... what sounds like relaxation and paradise for most of us, for Roman Hagara and Hans-Peter Steinacher it is "pretty tough," as they put it. A sailing regatta isn't a matter of a few minutes. When you are sailing hard to the wind there's no time for eating. Hence both of them usually return to land in the evening with a huge appetite.

"Many times we are alone at sea for weeks," they explain to Roland Trettl after arriving at the kitchen of Ikarus. "Without women. So you learn how to cook whether you like it or not." The fact that Hagara and Steinacher are no strangers to a stove was noted by the master chef because of the choice of dishes. You just don't prepare a zander filet in a toaster or microwave.

But first it's the appetizer's turn. For the soup Hans-Peter cuts one end of the beet into small square pieces and the rest into cubes of several centimeters (½"). A small suggestion from the chef: with this vegetable in particular you should always place some baking paper on the cutting board, "Otherwise you'll never get rid of the red stains."

Roland cuts the shallots and briefly braises them in oil inside a tall pot. Then he adds the beet cubes and pours vegetable broth over it. Once the beet has soft-boiled—about fifteen minutes—they are mashed and seasoned with vinegar, salt, and pepper.

Meanwhile, the horseradish cream is prepared with 1-2 tsp of creamy horseradish and a dash of salt warmed at low heat.

To prepare the soup, first the uncooked beet pieces are placed into the glass, then the pureed soup is added. Put the horseradish cream on the soup with a tablespoon and season with freshly ground horseradish and chives.

Teamwork is top priority for Roman and Hans-Peter.

ZANDER FILET

WITH MASHED POTATOES AND LEEK VEGETABLES

60 MINUTES

SCALE 7

INGREDIENTS ZANDER:
olive oil
800 g (28 oz) zander, salt
100 g (3½ oz) butter
2 thyme sprigs
3 garlic cloves
30 g (1 oz) capers
30 g (1 oz) breadcrumbs
30 g (1 oz) lemon filets and juice

MASHED POTATOES:
1 kg (2¼ lb) potatoes
salt, pepper, and nutmeg
100 g (3½ oz) butter
olive oil
130 g (4½ oz) milk
1 sprig of thyme
1 garlic clove

LEEK VEGETABLES:
2 stalks of leek
salt
50 g (1¾ oz) butter
600 g (21 oz) carrots
1/2 organic orange
1 sprig of tarragon
100 g (3½ oz) water

After this little warmup Roman Hagara and Hans-Peter Steinacher want to show their kitchen expertise with the zander filet. The fact that both of them are used to high standards is evident when they prepare the mashed potatoes. They decline the potato peeler offered by Roland Trettl to peel the pre-boiled potatoes. "We don't work with this thing. Would you happen to have a small knife?"

Roland is quick to fulfill their wish, contrary to the request of a food mill to strain the potatoes. The real pro still does it by hand.

While the three discuss the name of the food mill in French (Hans-Peter: "I thought you had a special term for each kichen item"), the potato mass is mixed with salt, pepper, ground nutmeg, French butter, olive oil, and finally with warm milk that Roland has boiled with some thyme and garlic.

For the leek vegetables, the master chef has preheated the kettle grill, where he now places the leek. After turning it over several times he seasons with salt, wraps it with a few slices of butter in aluminum foil, and puts it back on the grill for ten minutes.

Meanwhile, Roman and Hans-Peter peel the carrots and cut them into thin slices that are placed on the stove in a pan with the butter. After briefly braising them some orange peel is grated onto it for taste and the orange's juice is pressed into it. Then some salt and fresh tarragon are added and the carrots are stewed for ten minutes with 100 g (3½ oz) of water until they are nice and soft.

Now it's the turn of the zander. The following applies:

The first step for the perfect fish is plenty of olive oil.

It is heated in the pan. The zander itself is well salted before frying and the skin is perforated several times. Once the oil is quite hot the fish is placed into the pan. Butter, thyme, and garlic are added as well.

It is seasoned with lemon filets (extracted pulp) and some lemon juice.

Roman gets the honor of fileting the zander. The caper crust is placed on the filets with a spoon. Now the only thing left to do is remove the leek from the grill, then peel it and prepare it on the plate together with the carrots and the mashed potatoes. And finally, it's "Dinner's ready!"

Fish freaks: when they are at home, Roman and Hans-Peter get their fresh catch from a fisherman.

"It is important that the butter is foamy," Roland explains to his guests, who are surprised about how the fish is literally bathed in the oil-butter-spice blend. The Ikarus chef keeps adding with a spoon until the zander is done.

Now there's some rest for the fish as it drips off; however, the pan is still needed for later—for the crust of capers. The remaining butter and capers are heated in the pan. Once the butter has melted he adds breadcrumbs to form a firm mass.

Sabine Hagara and Christiane Steinacher are not about to miss this. The two wives have come to Salzburg to document the cooking session with their smartphones.

As good as their husbands might cook, it's not every day you can learn something from a star chef.

ALPINE SKIER

AUSTRIA
RESIDENCE: ANNABERG

MARCEL HIRSCHER

ROCK STAR FROM THE ALP.

NAME: Marcel Hirscher

BIRTHDAY: March 2, 1989

HEIGHT: 1.73 m (5' 7")

WEIGHT: 70 kg (154 lbs)

DISCIPLINE: slalom, giant slalom, Super-G

HOBBY: motocross

WEBSITE: www.marcelhirscher.at

FACEBOOK: www.facebook.com/hirschermarcel

He was all by himself on that Sunday in February 2013. Sure, there were over 50,000 people down there in the massive Schladming stadium waiting for him, all hoping that he would give them a victory—*the* victory. But up there at the start Marcel Hirscher was alone. Apart from the tremendous pressure weighing on him.

The ski nation of Austria was waiting for a gold medal until the very last World Cup race at home. Now he was the only one up there. And Marcel Hirscher did what he does best: he simply went for it, no mercy, his legs so fast they weren't even part of his body. GOLD!

Hirscher, who had always dreamed of being a rock star, will never forget bathing in the jubilant crowd. It was the emotional highlight of the comet-like ascent of this man who grew up in a Salzburg mountain village during the past several years. He won everything he could possibly win as a skier. Well, almost everything—you have to have some goals left.

2007

Junior World Championship - gold in giant slalom and silver in slalom

2008

Junior World Championship - gold in giant slalom and slalom

2009

First World Cup victory

2012

Winner Overall World Cup and Giant Slalom World Cup

2013

Winner Overall World Cup and Slalom World Cup; World Cup - gold in slalom & team, silver in giant slalom

"GIRLFRIEND, FAMILY, FANS - WITHOUT THESE PEOPLE MY VICTORIES WOULDN'T BE WORTH ANYTHING."

BEWARE OF SKI LODGES!

[INTERVIEW]

MARCEL, WHAT DO YOU EAT BETWEEN THE TWO RUNS OF A WORLD CUP SLALOM WHEN YOU ARE LEADING THE COMPETITION?

Whether it's a World Cup slalom or a regular World Cup race, there's no difference to me. I can eat even when I am nervous.
It's actually very important to eat something between the runs. This is of course limited to rather light and energy-rich items, such as energy bars, oats, and bananas.

INTERESTINGLY ENOUGH, THE SKI LODGES FOR HOBBY SKIERS SERVE MOSTLY HEARTY FOOD.

That's right (laughs). I have committed one or the other error during my semi-pro times. With goulash soup, spaghetti, or a frankfurter in your stomach you don't necessarily ski faster.
But as you increase your level you naturally make sure you are eating wholesome food.

WHAT WAS THE CRAZIEST THING YOU EVER ATE?

When we had a race in Japan as juniors I was housed with a guest family. They were really very nice, but when they started to suck the marrow from blueish-shimmering tiger prawns it was over for me.

WHAT WAS IT YOU COULDN'T STAND AS A CHILD? AND DO YOU LIKE IT TODAY?

I still have a difficult time with fish, even today. Now I like local fish, such as brook trout, but it has to be prepared really well. Too often you get something gooey that tastes like nothing.

TRY TO COMPARE YOUR SPORT TO A DISH. WHAT COMES TO MIND?

(thinks for a long time) Let's say you have many ingredients in a bowl, no matter what it is and what quality they are. You have to try to make something good from them. But all you have is yourself, your creativity, and good tools—that is, kitchen accessories.

WHAT CAN BE FOUND INSIDE YOUR FREEZER?

Half a spelt bread as a reserve, some scampi, and leaf spinach. Other than that not much, I really prefer to cook with fresh ingredients.

YOU ARE PLANNING A ROMANTIC DINNER WITH YOUR GIRLFRIEND: WHERE DOES IT TAKE PLACE?

It could actually be anywhere. Even at home in my own living room, as we travel enough already. The important thing is that we two are there.

THE LONG WAY TO THE TOP

A SALAD HAS MANY FACES.

Getting entirely different tastes with exactly the same ingredients—this is only possible with salad. "And that's because of the vinaigrette you use," says Roland Trettl. "You will be surprised how the character of a salad changes when you use a different dressing than the one you are used to." Need a few tips? Sure, no problem: see the section "The long way to the top SPECIAL" on pages 208/209.

SAUSAGE SALAD

WITH HOME FRIES

60 MINUTES

SCALE 4

INGREDIENTS:

350 g (12½ oz) baloney
2 scallions
8 radishes
10 cherry tomatoes
2 celery stalks
1 cucumber
1 TBSP chopped parsley
1 tsp chopped tarragon

VINAIGRETTE:

60 g (2 oz) white wine vinegar
1 TBSP mustard
1 TBSP creamy horseradish
salt and pepper
30 g (1 oz) pumpkin seed oil
60 g (2 oz) olive oil

HOME FRIES:

300 g (10½ oz) boiled potatoes
1 TBSP bacon cubes
1 TBSP chopped onion
20 g (¾ oz) olive oil
30 g (1 oz) butter
salt and pepper

If you are tracking Marcel Hirscher's success you have to get high: up to Stuhlalm lodge in Annaberg-Lungötz. In this idyllic, postcard-like landscape 1,467 meters (4,812 ft) above sea level, with the gigantic north face of the Bischofsmütze behind, the celebrated ski hero spent his childhood.

This is where little Marcel did his first cautious turns on the slope in front of his home. This is where his parents hosted hungry trekkers who had fought their way up from the valley during summer, looking for quiet and the perfect view that made it possible to take it easy regarding the sometimes silly problems of everyday life.

Only the best Austrian home cooking was on the menu. Marcel Hirscher still raves about the parental Kaiserschmarren—apparently there were guests who trekked up to Stuhlalm lodge just to treat themselves to it.

Cheese gnocchi was also part of the standard repertoire of the Hirscher family. And then there was the sausage salad, which today has to undergo a special test: does it taste as good as it does at home, on the wooden benches in front of the lodge some 1,000 meters (3,280 ft) lower?

A tremendous task for Roland Trettl, who encounters an experienced cook in his guest. "I graduated from the school of hotel management, so I am a trained cook and waiter," Marcel recounts—and with an air of excusing himself he adds, "Although I like to cook quite often, I can't do it on the level I used to."

The perfect technique at the cutting board is quite evident with the two-time World Cup winner and world champion. This is an advantage, as pretty much all of the ingredients are chopped up at the beginning of the cooking session.

Sausage, shallots, radish, cherry tomatoes, celery, and cucumber are chopped and placed in a bowl. Roland's concern about his guest cutting

"I've hurt myself more often while preparing skis."

himself badly and having to cancel his upcoming summer training camp in Chile is brushed aside:
he prefers to dedicate his attention to the boiled potatoes, which are peeled and cut into slices and braised in a pan with the cubed bacon and chopped parsley in some olive oil. Finally they are rinsed in butter.

"The butter is very important for the taste," says Hirscher. Roland stands next to him with crossed arms, nodding with satisfaction. "It's always fun to cook with people who are enthusiastic and who know what they are doing."

But the executive chef is not only a fan of Hirscher because of his cooking talents. "With skiing I like the wild dogs who are daring and don't just repeat the usual phrases. Alberto Tomba was one of them, and as an Italian I have always supported him. And you are one of those genuine characters." "You know what's appropriate for a host," Hirscher laughs, but he won't allow the praise to just sit there: "There's so many cool people in skiing. Felix Neureuther for example, or Aksel Lund Svindal. And there's some cool people on our Austrian team."

"Alright now, this is pretty sour!"

Now the sausage salad takes center stage again, as it wouldn't be tasty without the dressing. They use a small bowl to mix the white wine vinegar with mustard and creamy horseradish and add salt, pepper, pumpkin seed oil, and olive oil. Marcel has tasted it a bit too hastily. "Now wait," Roland replies, "we have to dilute it with water first; it won't be nearly as sour once it's in the salad."

After adding some 30 g (1 oz) of water the finished dressing is mixed with the sausage salad. The Ikarus chef adds parsley and tarragon before serving the sausage salad with the home fries on plates.

At the table it becomes pretty obvious that Marcel Hirscher can not only race down mountains at high speed. He's pretty fast with fork and knife, too. In the blink of an eye the sausage salad is gone—and going for seconds the World Cup winner also sets a record time.

"Looks like it's not too sour anymore," laughs Roland Trettl and receives a stern grin: "I'm having some more!"

Marcel Hirscher likes it down to earth: "It doesn't have to be salmon and caviar. A sausage salad is at least as delicious."

B.A.S.E. JUMPER &
FREESKIER

NORWAY
RESIDENCE: HEMSEDAL

KARINA HOLLEKIM

GET UP WHEN YOU ARE DOWN ON THE GROUND.

NAME: Karina Hollekim

BIRTHDAY: April 25, 1976

HEIGHT: 1.80 m (5' 9")

WEIGHT: 66 kg (145½ lbs)

DISCIPLINE: B.A.S.E., ski B.A.S.E., free ski

HOBBIES: skiing

WEBSITE: www.karinahollekim.com

"I am going to die." This was the last thought of Karina Hollekim before she crashed into a rock at 100 km/h (62 mph). During a show event in Switzerland the nightmare of every B.A.S.E. jumper became real for the Norwegian: her parachute did not open. Karina Hollekim suffered twenty-one open fractures in her legs and lost three liters (6 pints) of blood. She woke up in the hospital in unbearable pain. And with a smile. "Because the pain meant that I had survived!" The doctors announced that she would never be able to walk again, but Karina had a goal: at some time she wanted to ski once again. Four years and countless hours of training later, her dream came true: "When I did my first turn on fresh powder I felt like a small child. I just couldn't stop grinning." Today, Karina does lectures, she is an author, and she has published her autobiography on DVD.

2002

1. place World Championship Extreme Air, South Africa;
B.A.S.E. jump from the Perrine Bridge, USA

2004

1. place Red Bull Freeride
1. place Hemsedal Freeride, Norway
1. place Riksgränsen Freeride, Sweden
1. place Roldal Freeride Challenge, NOR

2005

First ski-B.A.S.E jump by a woman (from the "Lover's Leap" in Tahoe, USA)

2006

B.A.S.E. jump from Fatima's Hand, Mali

FILMS WITH KARINA HOLLEKIM

2009 *20 Seconds of Joy*
2009 *Extreme Air*
2007 *Anomaly*
2006 *Fatima's Hand*
2005 *4th Street*
2005 *Tangerine Dream*
2004 *Live a Little*
2003 *Override*

ROACHES FOR BREAKFAST.

[INTERVIEW]

WHAT MAKES YOUR DISCIPLINED ATHLETE'S HEART BECOME WEAK? WHAT DO YOU NEVER PICK UP WITH A FORK?

I love sushi, but I am quite picky about it. There's simply too much so-so or boring sushi around.
You'll never catch me with one of those classic prefabricated sushi boxes. To me that's sushi discrimination.

WHAT WAS YOUR GREATEST FAUX PAS WITH REGARDS TO NUTRITION BEFORE OR DURING A COMPETITION?

I always thought I liked Chinese food until I went to China. More to the point, until I went to Shanghai. During the days before the jump from the Jin Mao Tower I walked down the street one morning to look for some breakfast. In one of the shops I found a huge counter with small snacks. Too bad they weren't snacks, but all kinds of roasted bugs and roaches! I didn t need any breakfast after that and I lost six kilos (thirteen lbs) during my stay.

YOU HAVE ONE LAST MEAL. WHAT WOULD YOU ORDER?

I am a girl, so I have a weakness for chocolate. A perfect chocolate cake with fresh fruit and vanilla ice cream—that sounds like a really good finish.

HOW DO YOU PREPARE FOR YOUR JUMPS?

Before the actual jump I have visualized everything at least ten times. This helps me be prepared for any unexpected situations.

AND HOW DO YOU CELEBRATE VICTORIES?

In my life, success always goes with a glass of champagne (laughs).

YOUR PERSONAL RESTAURANT SUGGESTION?

There's a store in LA, I'd kill for its sushi! Okay, I will tell you the name: Nobu's. If you're ever there, don't miss it!

A VIEW INTO THE CRYSTAL BALL: WHAT COMES AFTER YOUR CAREER - MORE SIXPACK ABS OR SIX PACKS WITH BACON WRAP?

I might lose my fitness, but I certainly won't get fat. My body is way too important to me. If I don't eat well for a prolonged period or if I indulge in sweets I simply don't feel well. This doesn't mean that a burger can't at times make me happy, but overall I like to eat wholesome food and to take care of my body.

THE LONG WAY TO THE TOP

THREE-SECOND RULE.

The three-second rule can not only save the lives of motorists, but also the perfect taste of a fish dish. In case the fish is still raw inside—as in this case—simply fry it in hot oil for three seconds on each side and count twenty-one, twenty-two, twenty-three—and then get it out of the pan immediately!

EVERYBODY IS WAITING FOR KARINA:

The first date with Roland Trettl had to be canceled. There was a good reason for it—a ruptured appendix forced Karina to spend time in the hospital. But the Ikarus chef didn't know about it when this photo was taken.

TUNA THAI-STYLE

45 MINUTES

SCALE 7

INGREDIENTS:
350 g (12½ oz) tuna
4 scallops
sesame seeds (white and black), salt
100 g (3½ oz) glass noodles
olive oil, butter
lime juice

MARINADE:
30 g (1 oz) Dijon mustard
25 g (.85 oz) honey
20 g (¾ oz) soy sauce
20 g (¾ oz) sesame oil
1/2 organic lime

SAUCE:
30 g (1 oz) scallions
60 g (2 oz) celery
chili pod as desired
100 g (3½ oz) mango
1/2 lime
1 TBSP chili sauce
30 g (1 oz) cilantro
90 g (3 oz) sour cream
10 g (.35 oz) wasabi
Thai basil
50 g (1¾ oz) coconut milk
30 g (1 oz) soy sauce

You can make friends so quickly. When Karina Hollekim enters the Hangar-7 restaurant with her rudimentary Thai tuna recipe she gets a quizzical look from her host. "I don't understand," says Roland Trettl, scratching his head, "how is this supposed to work?"

But Hollekim knows how to grab the Ikarus chef by his sense of honor:

Do whatever you want with it. After all, I want to learn something from you.

A smile crosses Trettl's face—the instincts of the master chef are kicking into gear. "Come with me, I'll show you something!" With almost child-like anticipation he tells Karina what he has planned for her dish. Honey, mango, and scallops—these are the three ingredients he wants to utilize to "tune" Karina's recipe.

"But I've never prepared it like this," says Roland, and it sounds a bit like a forewarning. Karina's dry reply: "That's great. At our age it doesn't happen that often that we do something for the first time."

Trettl's mischievous grin says someone has catapulted right into the chef's heart. The spirit of improvisation and the will to try something new—this is what motivates the Ikarus chef to be at his best.

The marinade is quickly taken care of. All that is needed is to mix Dijon mustard with 1 tsp of honey, soy sauce, sesame oil, and the juice of half a lime in a bowl. To provide that special touch you can add some grated lime peel.

Now the tuna and scallops are soaked with the marinade, and generously so. "You are lucky, the scallops were delivered from Norway this morning," recounts Trettl and adds with pride: "30 kilos [66 lbs], I opened them all myself."

Then the tuna (not the scallops!) is rolled in a mix of black and white sesame seeds and ready for the pan. But that's for later.

The sauce that Karina and Roland get to work on now is slightly more elaborate. Both agree to a strict division of labor. Karina chops the scallion and the celery. Roland chops up two small strips of the chili pod, peels the mango, and cuts about ten finger-sized pieces into small cubes.

All of the ingredients are placed in a bowl and Roland adds the juice of half a lime once again while adding a TBSP of chili sauce. Cilantro must be part of it, although Trettl surprises with a tip that likely only a few hobby cooks know about: "Don't just use the leaves, add the stems as well. That's how they do it in Thailand," he tells Karina. To her surprised "Why?" he admits with a smile: "I forget why. But it tastes great."

To finish the sauce, sour cream, some wasabi, Thai basil, and a dash of coconut milk and soy sauce are added to the bowl and stirred well. After tasting it Karina is totally stoked. "Wow! I don't think I ever tasted something this good."
Flattered like that, Roland takes care

If Roland were pasta, by now he would be soft-boiled and wrapped around a finger.

of the glass noodles. It's a quick and simple procedure: heating salted water in a deep pan and boiling the noodles for about three minutes until they are soft. Meanwhile, Roland heats up the sauce in another pan until it is thick and creamy. Once the glass noodles are done they are strained and mixed with the sauce inside the pan.

Now the only thing left is the tuna and scallops. Roland heats plenty of olive oil in a pan. Karina is surprised: "I always use butter." "It's added later on, for the gravy," replies Roland. "The fish should be raw at the center, just like a good steak. And olive oil is better than butter."

The oil has to be piping hot before the fish is put into the pan. "This is the moment where you can destroy it all," laughs Karina.

But Roland has a foolproof method here

"If the fish gets burned you can forget about the whole dish."

as well. See "The long way to the top."

The last act of the dish is the gravy. Once the fish and scallops are done about two slices of butter are added to the pan with the hot oil. When it has melted some water is added and brought to a boil. The taste can be refined with some lime juice.

Now the tuna and scallops are basted with the gravy and served on the plate with the glass noodles.

"I have to say: I didn't think the dish could be improved this much," enthuses Karina. "Cooking with you is a unique experience."

And Roland blushes, like the tuna on the plate.

Pimp my tuna: Karina is delighted by Roland's recipe fine tuning.

KAYAKERS & CANOEISTS

SLOWAKIA
RESIDENCE: BRATISLAVA (DUKATOVÁ) AND
CZECHOSLOVAKIA
RESIDENCE: PRAGUE (HRADILEK)

JANA DUKATOVÁ & VAVRINEC HRADILEK

FROM THE RED STAR TO SUPERSTARS.

When their nation broke apart Jana Dukatová was in first grade, while "Vavra" Hradilek was still in kindergarten. Two decades later, the two of them have proven that a Czech-Slovakian cooperative can still be successful. During their training Jana—born in Bratislava—and Vavra—who grew up in Prague—push each other to top performance with resounding success. She has been the dominating woman athlete at the kayak World Cup competitions of the past years while he picked up a whitewater silver medal at the 2012 Olympic Games. Perhaps the reason this training duo works so well is the fact that they are rather different from each other. Jana gets her power from quiescence and also pocketed a degree in philosophy in addition to her achievements in sports. Vavra is a complete party animal who, according to his report, didn't sleep for five days after winning silver in London.

NAME Jana Dukatová
BIRTHDAY: June 13, 1983
HEIGHT: 1.80 m (5' 9")
WEIGHT: 65 kg (143 lbs)
DISCIPLINE: whitewater kayak, canoe-slalom
HOBBIES: windsurfing, snowboarding and reading
WEBSITE: www.janadukatova.sk

2006
World Champion-gold (kayak)

2009
Overall World Cup winner (kayak)

2010
Overall World Cup winner (kayak); World Champion-gold (canoe); European Champion-gold (kayak); World Champion-silver (kayak); European Champion-silver (canoe)

2011
Overall World Cup winner (kayak); World Champion-gold (kayak, team); World Champion-silver (kayak)

NAME: Vavrinec Hradilek
NICKNAME: Vavra
BIRTHDAY: March 10, 1987
HEIGHT: 1.68 m (5' 5")
WEIGHT: 75 kg (165 lbs)
DISCIPLINE: whitewater kayak
HOBBIES: paddle boarding, surfing
WEBSITE: www.vavrahradilek.cz

2007
World Champion-bronze (team)

2009
World Champion-gold (team)

2010
World Champion-silver
European Champion-bronze

2011
2. place Overall World Cup

2012
Olympic-silver

Vavra's biggest enemy sits in his boat: he has been suffering from asthma since birth. But high-performance sports have never been an obstacle for him; rather, they are a way to keep his condition in check.

Jana's first whitewater race ended in the hospital: she had an enormous cut on her head after hitting a rock.

THE CRUX WITH THE POTATO.

[INTERVIEW]

WHAT MAKES YOUR DISCIPLINED ATHLETE'S HEART WEAK? WHAT WOULD YOU NEVER PICK UP WITH A FORK?

Vavra: With food I pretty much can't resist anything. I love Czech food—too bad it's extremely heavy, though.

Jana: I also like the traditional kitchen a lot, but with seafood the fun is over for me.

WHAT WAS YOUR BIGGEST MISTAKE REGARDING NUTRITION BEFORE OR DURING A COMPETITION?

Vavra: When you say "potato" in Czech it also means "fourth place." I've tried it twice before a competition, and it's actually true! Hence, never again potatoes!

Jana: Tuna pasta. I had it once, never again!

WHAT DO THE EVENINGS AND THE MORNING BEFORE A COMPETITION LOOK LIKE? WHAT'S ON YOUR PLATES?

Jana: Something sweet, that's important. Back then I was always too nervous before races, but with chocolate I have my nerves under control.

Vavra: A good steak for dinner before a competition is always a good move.

HOW DO YOU CELEBRATE A SUCCESSFUL COMPETITION?

Vavra: Well, after my silver medal in London it was pretty serious. As my race happened early at the start of the Olympic Games, I really took advantage of this event. For the first five days I was going around everywhere and didn't bat an eye (laughs).

Jana: Crazy, I'm fine with some mojitos (laughs).

IS THERE A SPECIAL PLACE OR A RESTAURANT WHERE YOU WANT TO HAVE LUNCH OR DINNER?

Jana: All I can say is dinner in Paris. I love French food, not to mention their wine.

Vavra: I know a great restaurant in my hometown of Prague, in the largest building in the city, with a great view.

YOU HAVE ONE LAST MEAL. WHAT WOULD YOU ORDER?

Vavra: I would most likely be way too nervous to eat anything ...

Jana: Well, I would come up with something. Most likely a traditional dish from home, such as duck with cabbage, potatoes, and dumplings.

A LOOK INTO THE CRYSTAL BALL: WHAT COMES AFTER YOUR CAREER - MORE SIXPACK ABS OR ABS WITH A BACON COAT?

Vavra: I know my body. As soon as I stop training I explode (laughs), so I hope I will continue to practice sports.

Jana: In my case it's the opposite. I even tried to gain weight once, but it didn't work.

THE LONG WAY TO THE TOP

DULL CUCUMBER?

Cucumbers are a delicious and wholesome side dish, but they can actually destroy a dish if you don't take necessary precautions. "Cucumbers have a lot of water," explains Roland Trettl. "If you don't get rid of it before cooking the whole dish might taste dull." To enjoy their full taste, cucumbers should be salted and left for ten minutes. The rest is automatic. You'll see!

EURO-MEXICAN WRAPS

60 MINUTES

SCALE 6

INGREDIENTS:
2 roast beef steaks
(250 g [8¾ oz] each)
salt, pepper
2 red onion
2 yellow bell peppers
15 oyster mushrooms
olive oil, salt, pepper
wraps

GUACAMOLE:
2 avocados
salt, chili powder
cilantro
1 TBSP lime juice

SAUCE:
1 red bell pepper
1 red onion
2 tomatoes
1 garlic clove
parsley
1 TBSP lime juice
salt, pepper, olive oil

SOUR CREAM-CUCUMBER SAUCE:
1 cucumber
200 g (7 oz) sour cream
salt, chili

A typical Mexican dish prepared by a South Tyrolian, a Czech, and a Slovakian. Can it turn out okay? "What we are doing here," says Roland Trettl, "you'll never find in Mexico anyway. This is pretty much the European version with cucumber and mushroom —and without beans."

"That's how it's supposed to be," enthuses Vavra Hradilek, "we blend two cultures and make the best of what the two have to offer." He and his training colleague are used to improvising anyway. "While we are on tour," recounts Jana, "there's often ten of us living in the same house. There's plenty of guys there—and none of them knows how to cook."

"That's why we have these wraps quite often, they are so easy to prepare," adds Vavra and turns to Roland: "I'm anxious to see what else you can show us!" "Well, let's get started with the guacamole ..."

Roland removes the pits of two avocados and uses a spoon to carve out the pulp. He mashes the avocados with a fork so a creamy mass is created and seasons with salt and some chili. Finally some cilantro and lime juice—done ...

Next is the salsa sauce. Jana and Vavra chop the bell pepper and onion and cube the tomatoes and put them in a bowl together with the pressed garlic clove and parsley. "Something sour can't be bad," remarks Roland and adds some lime juice. Then he adds salt, pepper, and some olive oil and stirs.

Time to take care of the third bowl, which is still empty. It's going to be filled with a sour cream-cucumber sauce. And its preparation is as simple as it sounds.

While Roland and Vavra talk animately about chili and its varying spiciness Jana peels the cucumber and cuts it into small pieces. They are then placed on a plate and salted and allowed to rest (see "The long way to the top"). After a few minutes Roland mixes the cucumber pieces with a pot of sour cream and seasons the resulting sauce with salt and chili.

Meanwhile, one of Roland's cooks at Ikarus has fired up the grill.

... Vavra laughs. "No no, of course this can be done in a pan," Roland replies. "But this special charcoal taste can't

"Okay, so for this dish you need a garden" ...

be replaced. So when you have the necessary equipment, I suggest using a grill."

Roland adds coarse salt to each side of the beef while Jana and Vavra look at each other incredulously. Does this guy really grill indoors? Right here in the ki ...?

They haven't finished their thought and the meat is already sizzling on the grill. These are the moments the master chef enjoys the most. With a triumphant smile he cuts a few large onion and bell pepper slices, places them on the grill, and puts on the lid.

Kitchen luxury: each ingredient requires its own container for the wraps.

"How do you like your meat?," he asks them. "Bloody!," replies Vavra with much conviction "Usually it's well-done, but today it can be somewhat less," says Jana.

And then the pan still gets a workout. That is, frying the oyster mushrooms in hot olive oil. A delicious side dish—the only thing to add here is salt. Since Jana is a bit too hesitant for Roland's taste the chef announces:

"Hit it! You can't over-salt it."

Finally, the only thing left to do is briefly bake the wraps. Roland puts them into a moist dishtowel—"so they don't dry out too much"—and puts them on the grill. Meanwhile, he cuts the grilled meat into small pieces. After a few minutes everything is ready for a meal where manual dexterity is required. And creativity, because the way you fill and eat these wraps is entirely up to you.

SOCCER PLAYER

AUSTRIA
RESIDENCE: TRABZON, TURKEY

MARC JANKO

THE MAN WITH THE GOLDEN FOOT.

NAME: Marc Janko

BIRTHDAY: June 25, 1983

HEIGHT: 1.96 m (6' 4")

WEIGHT: 93 kg (205 lbs)

POSITION: striker

HOBBIES: music, golf, tennis, poker, beach volleyball, badminton, snooker

WEBSITE: www.marcjanko.com

TWITTER: @JankoMarc

FACEBOOK: www.facebook.com/MarcJanko

His mother won the bronze medal at the Olympic Games. His father was the Austrian high jump champion. These are good qualifications for offspring, but they are certainly no guarantee of a career as a sportsman. The fact that the conversion of chances is one of the most outstanding strengths of Marc Janko was proven by this model athlete when he entered professional soccer. The major break came for the Viennese with the Red Bull Salzburg team. He quickly became a crowd favorite because of his goal instinct.

Apart from the three championships with the team Marc Janko established one goal record after another, and by now he is a fixture of the Austrian National Team. One highlight of his career were the thirty-nine league goals during the 2008/2009 season that earned him the Bronze Boot as the third-best goal scorer of all the European leagues. His stints abroad with Twente Enschede, FC Porto, and Trabzonspor have brought maturity to Marc Janko. His goal instinct has traveled with him. The score of this striker is impressive no matter the league.

THE BIGGEST VICTORIES:

3 x Austrian Champion: 2007, 2009, 2010
1 x Dutch Cup Champion: 2011
2 x Dutch Supercup Champion: 2010, 2011
1 x Portuguese Champion: 2012
1 x Portuguese Supercup Champion: 2012

AWARDS:

1 x Austrian Top Scorer: 2009
1 x Bronze Boot (UEFA): 2009
1 x The World's most effective Top Division Goal Scorer (IFFHS): 2009
1 x The World's best Top Division Goal Scorer (IFFHS): 2009
1 x APA-Soccer Player of the Year 2008

You can learn a lot in soccer, except goal instinct. Marc Janko has it, no doubt about it. Spectacular goals in international arenas are a trademark of this striker who is as tall as a tree.

GUT INSTINCT AS A RECIPE FOR SUCCESS.

[INTERVIEW]

WHICH FAMOUS SPORTSMAN/ SPORTSWOMAN WOULD YOU LIKE TO HAVE DINNER WITH?

Michael Jordan. With his charisma he has caught peoples' imaginations far beyond his sport; he has brought basketball to people who never had anything to do with it. And he has inspired me a lot.

THE TASTE OF YOUR CHILDHOOD IS ...

... sweet! One sweet dish in particular comes to my mind: strawberries with cream. My grandmother always made it for the kids. Simple but very tasty.

BEER IN THE GARDEN OR A GLASS OF WINE AT THE BAR?

The garden, with friends, because it's more casual.

WHAT WAS THE CRAZIEST THING YOU EVER ATE?

It wasn't that long ago. I was in Rome with my girlfriend at a very, very good restaurant. They had half-raw pigeon—apparently a delicacy in Italy. I couldn't even eat half of it ...

WHAT WAS IT YOU COULDN'T STAND AS A CHILD? AND DO YOU LIKE IT TODAY?

Almost every kind of vegetable, particularly spinach—I just couldn't stand it. But today it's one of my favorite dishes.

AT THE TABLE WITH FAMILY AND FRIENDS: ARE YOU THE FIRST ONE TO FINISH THEIR PLATE OR DO YOU ENJOY EVERY BITE?

I'd be somewhere in the middle. Although my girlfriend would probably protest, she says I am a "gobbler" (grins).

YOU ARE PLANNING A ROMANTIC DINNER FOR TWO: WHERE DOES IT TAKE PLACE?

At a quiet open space with a nice view. With plenty of candles—I love candlelight!

WHICH CHARACTERISTIC UNITES A SUCCESSFUL SOCCER PLAYER WITH A GOOD COOK?

Feeling! I don't refer to the feel for the ball here but the feel for the situation. I act by following my gut feeling; for example, in standard situations in the penalty area I do unconventional things and go to locations where others wouldn't. In many cases the ball actually comes my way.

YOU WAKE UP IN THE MIDDLE OF THE NIGHT WITH THE MUNCHIES. WHAT HAS TO BE IN YOUR FRIDGE?

Wild boar sausage from Styria, the home of my girlfriend. Chocolate. And grana-padano cheese.

TRY TO COMPARE YOUR SPORT WITH A DISH. WHICH ONE COMES TO MIND?

Burgers hit it pretty much right-on. There's a bit of everything in there—a good mix. Endurance, technique, strategy.

COOKING IS ...

... passion, relaxation, fun. And most of all, pleasure.

THE LONG WAY TO THE TOP

POTATO SALAD: IT DOESN'T HAVE TO BE ALWAYS POTATOES.

A potato salad without potatoes? It works with the topinambour—the original potato. Roland recommends the tuber even to dedicated potato fans as a tasty variation. Topinambour contains less starch but more protein. Its aroma is similar to artichokes. The tubers can be used raw for salads, for example. They can also be boiled in saltwater. But beware: contrary to potatoes, due to their thin skin they can't be stored as long.

BURGERS

WITH MEDITERRANEAN POTATO SALAD

60 MINUTES

SCALE 6

INGREDIENTS:
80 g (2¾ oz) white bread
milk
170 g (6 oz) onions
80 g (2¾ oz) butter
90 g (3 oz) ham
10 g (1/3 oz) parsley
1 garlic clove
400 g (14 oz) veal
300 g (10½ oz) pork
2 eggs
mustard

POTATO SALAD:
400 g (14 oz) potatoes
15 cherry tomatoes
3 shallots
10 basil leaves
60 g (2 oz) olive oil
2 green tomatoes
1 small young zucchini
1 avocado
2 TBSP roasted pine nuts
70 g (2 1/3 oz) white balsamic vinegar
chili powder
1 TBSP mustard
pepper
lemon juice
salt

Marc Janko was clearly disadvantaged by the referee even before his cooking season kicked off: his wish for Kaiserschmarrn (sugared pancake with raisins) was rejected because this position was already taken for the compilation of this cookbook for athletes. The Austrian National Team striker chose his second favorite dish: burgers.

Right at the beginning of the first half, the preparation of the burger ...

... there's a sharp slide tackle from the master chef: "Can you cook at all?" Somebody else might have been impressed by this rough kind of play, but not so the captain of the National Team, who has learned how to persevere in the heated atmosphere of Southern European cities. "Actually, quite well. But you know, Roland, there have to be those carrying the piano and those who play it. Regarding cooking, I belong the latter group." This counterstrike shows some effect on his counterpart, who hands the winner of the Bronze Boot the bread slices to soak them in a bowl of milk. Meanwhile, Roland Trettl braises the chopped onions in a small pan with some butter, cuts bacon, parsley, and the garlic clove, and then elegantly brings the striker back into the game: Janko squeezes the bread and blends it with the ingredients prepared by Trettl.

Then the meat mixture is passed through the meat grinder. To bind the now-thin meat, 2 eggs and 1 TBSP of mustard are added and mixed thoroughly by hand. According to Trettl this is very important: the meat should not be too firm nor too loose. Not entirely unfounded, Marc Janko asks whether there isn't some better definition or some sort of gradation. The master chef of Ikarus thinks this over for some time and then he gives his answer, one which brings every cooking apprentice to desperation but satisfies a striker who earns his living with his intuition: a matter of gut feeling. The fact that Trettl's feeling is right on is evident when the palm-sized hamburgers are shaped.

Kickoff for the second half time: the Mediterranean potato salad.

Now the hamburger is given a timeout. The two chefs enter the second half and tackle the potato salad. Janko gets a knife handed to him to peel the boiled potatoes, as Trettl is of the opinion that the talent of a cook is evident when peeling potatoes. This causes Janko to laugh. "As a child and teen I used to play in the woods a lot, and I always had a pocket knife with me. My talent is limited to handling knives. Regarding cooking, I am just on the regional league level."

More ingredients are chopped up by Marc: he first cuts the potatoes, then the olives, cherry tomatoes, and shallots. The latter are lightly braised in a little olive oil. The green tomatoes—they have a firmer bite than their red colleagues—are also sliced thinly, just like the young zucchini. All of the ingredients are mixed in a bowl and shallots and pine nuts are added last. Trettl seasons the potato salad with white balsamic vinegar, which has a fresher aroma and is less sweet than its dark relative. Olive oil, a dash of chili powder, 1 TBSP of mustard, and pepper round off the taste. Just before serving Trettl adds a dash of lemon juice as well as salt to the potato salad.

A few dashes of Mediterranean: lemon juice and white balsamic vinegar add summer freshness to the potato salad.

The hot phase of overtime: the burgers go into the pan.

"Which pan?" would be the question of some readers looking at the photos of the grill. When the sun came out after a prolonged time in Salzburg the two athlete cooks decided to move the last phase of the preparation to the outdoor lounge of Hangar-7. But the easier way to prepare the burgers is using a pan, so this method will be explained here.

"I can cook pretty well. Let's say, regional league. With respect to eating I am world-class." - Marc Janko

To not burn anything during the decisive phase of the match, simply follow Trettl's frying tactic:

1. Heat oil in a pan.

2. Fry the burgers. Put some butter onto the top side.

3. Flip them only once!

4. After flipping them, add butter to the pan—if you like, use herb butter.

5. Lower the heat so the burgers don't get burned.

ALPINE
SNOWBOARDER

AUSTRIA
RESIDENCE: WILHELMSBURG

BENJAMIN KARL

AFTER OLYMPIA IS BEFORE OLYMPIA.

NAME: Benjamin Martin Karl

NICKNAME: Benny

BIRTHDAY: October 16, 1985

HEIGHT: 1.86 m (6' 1")

WEIGHT: 87 kg (192 lbs)

DISCIPLINE: parallel slalom, parallel giant slalom

HOBBIES: mountainbiking, canyoning

WEBSITE: www.benjamin-karl.com

Benny Karl knew how to ski before he could talk. His mother put him on planks when he was two years old and played a decisive role in that from then on, the Austrian's passion would be snow and the mountains. Climbing mountains, skiing, trekking, and finally, snowboarding. Today, he sports an Olympic silver medal, four World Champion titles, and many World Cup victories as part of his long list of achievements. Benny is married to Nina, the daughter of former Austrian ski racer Werner Grissmann, and has a daughter.

2005

Junior Champion parallel giant slalom/ snowboard; European Cup Overall Winner

2008

1. World Cup winner
1. Overall World Cup Victory

2009

Parallel Giant Slalom Champion

2010

Overall World Cup winner: Olympic silver in Vancouver

2011

Two-time parallel Slalom and Parallel Giant Slalom World Champion

2013

Parallel Giant Slalom Champion

"A WILD GUY, BRAZEN AND FAST!"

THE RYE BREAD PRIVILEGE.

[INTERVIEW]

WHAT MAKES YOUR DISCIPLINED ATHLETE'S HEART WEAK? WHAT DO YOU NEVER PICK UP WITH A FORK?

Chips and french fries are out of the question. Now, sweets are a totally different issue. I don't mind two pieces of cake now and then. When there's sweet rolls half of them disappear in no time ...

WHAT WAS YOUR GREATEST FAUX PAS REGARDING NUTRITION BEFORE OR DURING A COMPETITION?

That really doesn't happen with us snowboarders. Particularly with overseas competitions we have to eat whatever they are serving us. And it's more likely that we don't eat enough ... (laughs) ... and then the next day we are too weak because we didn't eat enough.

WHAT DOES THE EVENING AND THE MORNING BEFORE A COMPETITION LOOK LIKE? WHAT'S ON YOUR PLATE AND IN YOUR GLASS?

There's really no routine. As I said: we eat whatever they put in front of us. The one dish that's most common when abroad is oatmeal or an egg dish. I keep noticing Austria has the best food by far. Take something like rye bread—totally standard for us—it is unknown elsewhere ...

HOW DO YOU CELEBRATE A SUCCESSFUL COMPETITION?

With friends, beer, and Vodka Bull. In that precise order.

LET'S ASSUME YOU GET A DATE WITH LINDSEY VONN FOR DINNER. WHERE WOULD YOU TAKE HER?

The finest and reportedly the best place is at home, so where else could it be for two Red Bull athletes if not at Hangar-7?

YOU HAVE ONE LAST MEAL. WHAT WOULD YOU ORDER?

(without the slightest hesitation) Bacon-dumpling soup. Beef tartar. Steak with pepper sauce. Apple strudel with vanilla ice cream. And an espresso ...

A LOOK INTO THE CRYSTAL BALL: WHAT COMES AFTER YOUR CAREER - MORE SIXPACK ABS OR A SIX PACK WITH BACON WRAP?

We athletes tend to be pretty vain with our bodies ... but let me think about it ... Okay: if I go on TV and don't have time to eat then I'll stay slim. Otherwise I'd be like Roland ... that's more like bacon-wrapped six pack ... (laughs)

THE LONG WAY TO THE TOP

CUT AT THE ROOT.

Onions can be chopped more conveniently and, most importantly, evenly when you leave the end of the root while cutting. This keeps the layers and fibers together and they can be removed with precision!

PEPPER STEAK

WITH POTATO GRATINS AND PORCINI

80 MINUTES

SCALE 8

INGREDIENTS:
4 beef filets (about 240 g [8½ oz])
40 g (1 1/3 oz) olive oil
40 g (1¼ oz) butter
1 sprig of thyme
1 sprig of rosemary
1 garlic clove

GRATIN:
350 g (12 oz) milk
150 g (5 oz) cream
1 garlic clove
1 sprig of thyme
500 g (17½ oz) potatoes
50 g (1¾ oz) Parmesan
salt and pepper
nutmeg

SAUCE:
50 g (1¾ oz) butter
1 shallot
1 TBSP cognac
Madeira
150 g (5 oz) veal stock (jus)
10 g (1/3 oz) pickled green pepper
2 TBSP whipped cream

PORCINI:
500 g (17½ oz) porcini
20 g (¾ oz) olive oil
30 g (1 oz) butter
1 TBSP old balsamic vinegar
lime juice
1 TBSP chopped parsley
salt and pepper

Uncertainty—even just a hint of it—and Roland Trettl are two terms that exclude each other. Usually. Because when Benny Karl announces right from the start with his mischievous grin that he's waiting to see whether Roland's pepper steak will beat the one made by Werner Grissmann, the time has come. "Great, now I am worried about the pepper sauce" was the semi-serious reply of Ikarus's executive chef.

"The Grissmann* family introduced me to good cooking. And the pepper steak prepared by Grizzly (Note: W. Grissmann's nickname) was the starting point. Once you have a really great one you're sold," recounts Benny Karl while Roland Trettl blends milk and cream, preparing the sauce for the potato gratin.

After adding garlic and thyme the sauce is strained through a sieve and seasoned with salt, pepper, and nutmeg. "Generally, potatoes have to be soft, so I always use Asia graters to get a consistent thickness of the slices (2 cm [¾"])."

Trettl adds two layers of potato slices and some sauce to the dish. Then he grates Parmesan over the potatoes. "The French would never do this, but it binds the sauce," he adds. He repeats the procedure until the soufflé dish is full. Now the gratin is placed in the oven at 180 degrees (350°F) for one hour.

Now it's the filet's turn. To stabilize the flanks Trettl wraps thread around the steaks. He anticipates Benny's inquisitive look: "You don't have to, it's a cosmetic thing."

Meanwhile, he preheats the oven to 90 degrees (200°F). He then adds olive oil

to the pan. The steaks are briefly fried at high temperature on both sides until they feature a nice crust. While the meat sizzles and hisses, Trettl adds butter, thyme, rosemary, and a mashed garlic clove to round off the taste.

Then he puts the steaks in the oven for about twenty minutes. Benny has meanwhile tasted a few treats from the current menu offered by sous chef Tomy and is wide awake and ready. "Why in the oven and not in the pan until they're done?" "Because if you do then you might have a nice crust but the inside is still raw. But in the oven everything is cooked nice and even without becoming dry," Trettl replies.

To take advantage of the roasted aroma of the steak the pepper sauce is now prepared in the same pan. Chopped shallots are braised in butter until soft. Cognac is added and singed. After adding a dash of Madeira and the veal jus the sauce simmers for about two minutes at low temperature before the green pepper is added. To make the sauce more creamy Trettl adds cream to the sauce towards the end. Meanwhile, the porcini are fried in olive oil and butter and are seasoned with balsamic vinegar, a dash of lime juice, parsley, salt, and pepper.

It doesn't get any fresher: Benny and Roland pick up ingredients at the market.

*Werner Grissmann—Austrian skiing legend of the 1970's, world champion in sarcasm, and Benny's father-in-law—actually believes he has taught Eckart Witzigmann—the chef of the century—how to cook. Witzigmann in turn was Trettl's master. So the conditions for a cooking competition at the highest level are given.

FENCER

UKRAINE
RESIDENCE: MYKOLAJIW

OLGA KHARLAN

ALMOST EVERYTHING THAT SHINES IS GOLD.

NAME: Olga Kharlan

BIRTHDAY: September 4, 1990

HEIGHT: 1.71 m (5' 6")

WEIGHT: 65 kg (143 lbs)

DISCIPLINE: saber

HOBBYS: films, pop music, shopping

Where others have their photos from vacation trips or family pictures, Olga Kharlan's place is shiny and sparkles. Her apartment is truly a unique collection of trophies and medals. No wonder, the twenty-three-year-old Ukrainian has won almost as many medals as she has birthdays. And it doesn't look like this will change in the coming years. And the only reason Olga Kharlan came to fencing was because her parents couldn't afford expensive dance lessons anymore and the fencing lessons were free. "Good for me," says Olga today. Otherwise, the world would have one less absolutely top class athlete.

2008

Olympian Gold (Team)

2009

WC-Gold (Team)
WC-Silver (Single)
EC -Gold (Single & Team)

2010

WC-Silver (Single & Team)
EC-Gold (Team)

2011

WC-Bronze (Single)
WC-Silver (Team)
EC -Gold (Single)
Universiade-Gold (Single)

2012

Olympic Games-Bronze (Single)
EC-Gold (Single)
WC-Silver (Team)
EC-Silver (Team)

2013

WC-Gold (Single)
WC-Gold (Team)
EC-Gold (Single)
EC-Silver (Team)

*WC-World Championship **EC-European Championship

"YOU ALWAYS HAVE TO BE ONE STEP AHEAD OF YOUR ENEMY. IF YOU'RE NOT, THEN HE IS."

SUCCESSFUL WITH AN EMPTY STOMACH.

[INTERVIEW]

WHAT MAKES YOUR DISCIPLINED ATHLETE'S HEART WEAK? WHAT DO YOU NEVER PICK UP WITH A FORK?

I believe I am one of the few people who can't stand chocolate. On the other hand, I would die for Japanese food—I can always have some sushi. And of course I love the food of my home country, Ukraine.

WHAT DO THE EVENING AND MORNING BEFORE A COMPETITION LOOK LIKE IN YOUR CASE? WHAT'S ON YOUR PLATE AND IN YOUR GLASS?

For breakfast there's only coffee and perhaps a croissant, nothing else after that. No lunch, even if the competition is in the afternoon. I always get to the start with an empty stomach.

YOU HAVE ONE LAST MEAL. WHAT WOULD YOU ORDER?

Smoked fish, seafood, and sushi, of course.

WHO ARE THE THREE PEOPLE SITTING AT THE TABLE OF YOUR PERFECT DINNER?

Well, first I would invite Mariel Zagunis. She is one of my toughest competitors and at the same time a wonderful person from whom I have learned a whole lot. Apart from that I would be interested in athletes who leave a mark on their sport with their performance, such as Lionel Messi or Usain Bolt.

WHAT WAS THE CRAZIEST THING YOU EVER ATE?

Snails. I actually didn't want to eat them at all—I pity them the way they crawl around slowly (laughs). Then one day I was talked into it and I hated it.

AT THE TABLE WITH FAMILY AND FRIENDS: ARE YOU THE FIRST ONE TO FINISH YOUR PLATE OR DO YOU ENJOY EVERY BITE?

That depends on the situation. When I am at training camp I always eat as fast as possible to have some time for other things. But when I am off I enjoy going out with friends to dinner and chatting. In this case it may take a long time for me to finish my plate.

TRY TO COMPARE YOUR SPORT WITH A DISH. WHAT COMES TO MIND?

It would have to be spicy and get you sweating, that's for sure. Off the top of my head I can only think of kimchi, a typical Korean dish I like very much.

THE LONG WAY TO THE TOP

THE "BLOOD" OF THE BEET.

If you cook beets you should always leave the vegetable in one piece. Roland Trettl: "Never peel or cut off the trunk. Otherwise the blood will seep out." In other words, beets will lose their beautiful color. The only thing red would be the water.

BORSCHT BATTLE.

ROLAND TRETTL VS. OLGA KHARLAN

We might have seen this phenomenon at work in politics: controversy starting at the base. But things can also become complicated in a kitchen when two minds think differently. More precisely: the base of the Borscht. Even if prepared by a master chef.

She only needs two words to turn the expectant grin on Roland Trettl's face into a scandalized snort: "Too salty."

For five hours he had cooked the beef with the beets, carrots, and celery in saltwater until soft. The base was a beautiful red; he had even added a laurel leaf. And now this. "Too salty?! I never heard that one before!"

And Kharlan isn't even done with her counterpart—not yet. The fencer prepares the all-important blow. "With my mom at home the base is never red." Pow! A direct hit ...

"Now that's enough," bursts out Trettl with faked indignation, and just like that produces two large pots that he places next to each other on the stove. "We make two versions. Yours and mine."

Let the Borscht battle begin!

5 HOURS OF PREPARATION

120 MINUTES

SCALE **8**

INGREDIENTS:
400 g (14 oz) beef shoulder
3 marrow bone
350 g (12 1/3 oz) beets
3 onions
50 g (1¾ oz) red bell pepper
90 g (3 oz) tomatoes
2 carrots
100 g (3½ oz) white cabbage
olive oil
200 g (7 oz) potatoes
80 g (3 oz) heavy sour cream
pepper, salt
1 tsp dill
1 garlic clove
1 l (4¼ cups) water
20 g (¾ oz) rice vinegar
1 laurel leaf
sugar

GARLIC BREAD:
rye bread
garlic
salted butter

[OLGA & ROLAND]

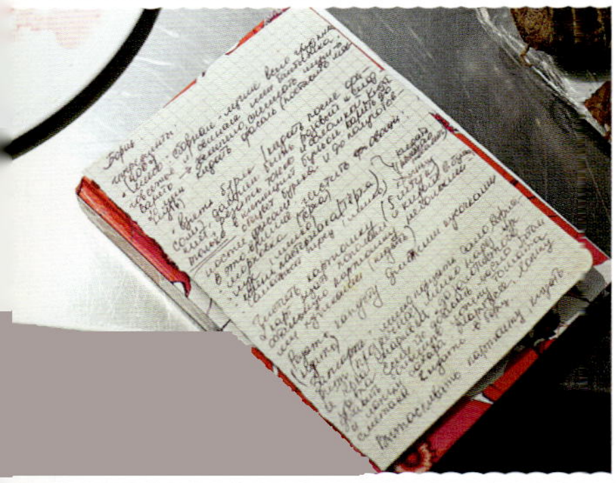

CLEAR THE RING

"This will be the best Borscht of your life," teases Roland while peeling the raw potatoes and chopping the beef into cubes and the beets into finger-sized slices. Olga cooly replies: "You'll have to take this up with my family."

The Ukrainian has brought along her sister Tatjana as reinforcement, who is busy rummaging through her bag, looking for the original recipe. Roland laughs: "And on top of it you're cheating!"

But what is it made of, this Borscht base à la Kharlan? The answer is as surprising as it is simple: saltwater. "The color and the taste are the result of cooking," Olga explains while ignoring the master chef's skeptic look.

No matter which base you want to cook at home—whether Roland's more elaborate or Olga's Ukranian version—the following suggestions apply to both of them:

Boil the beef cubes, marrowbone, and beets with the chosen base and allow to simmer vigorously while covered.

Meanwhile, cube the onion, bell pepper, and tomatoes, grate the carrots into slices, and cut the white cabbage into long strips.

Roland fries all of the ingredients in a deep pan with some oil before he adds a little juice of the base and allows it to simmer at medium heat.

Once the liquid in the pan has evaporated, the contents and the raw potatoes, together with the beef and the beets, are put into the still boiling base. Allow the boiling to continue until the potatoes are nice and soft.

While waiting, Olga and her sister Tatjana philosophize about their traditional dish: "There's so many different kinds of Borscht in the Ukraine, almost every family has its own recipe." Roland smiles: "That's just like our Christmas goose. Mom's goose is always the best one. That is why I would never prepare a Christmas goose in my restaurant: I could only come out losing."

Sister act: Olga Kharlan brought her sister Tatjana along. Including the "pony" of mom Kharlan (bottom left) is present.

BELL!

The Borscht competition reaches its decisive phase; Roland and Olga add 2 TBSP of heavy sour cream and stir and then season their dishes. One more dash of salt over here, some dill over there. Note: only a well-seasoned Borscht is a good Borscht.

Roland now cuts the rye bread. Olga rubs the slices first with a garlic clove and then adds salted butter. The bread is put into the oven at 200 degrees (350°F), where it is baked until it is nice and crusty.

THE FINISH

The two Borscht dishes are prepared in a bowl with the baked garlic bread served as the side dish.

But the expected combat turns into a friendly handshake. "Tastes really great," the master chef praises the fencer's Borscht. She in turn is convinced by Roland's Borscht, too. "I love it!"

"Although both dishes are similar they taste entirely different," analyzes Roland. What to do? "We agree it's a tie," Olga suggests.

And this will certainly satisfy mom Kharlan as well.

CLIMBER

AUSTRIA
RESIDENCE: INNSBRUCK

DAVID LAMA

SUMMITEER. PIONEER. CHILD PRODIGY.

NAME: David Lama

NICKNAME: Fuzzy

BIRTHDAY: August 4, 1990

HEIGHT: 1.70 m (5' 5")

WEIGHT: 58 kg (190 lbs)

HOBBIES: biking, traveling, skiing, photography

WEBSITE: www.david-lama.com

David Lama is regarded as the trailblazer of a new generation of climbers. This might be due to the fact he was able to look at the mountains of Tirol from his cradle. Or perhaps because he inherited a love of mountains from his father, a Nepalese mountain guide. David Lama began his career as a climber at five years old. A short time later he was the youth champion and the youngest double European Champion in the history of the sport. At seventeen he had enough of climbing gyms and competitions; adventures out in nature were beckoning. Ever since then David Lama has worked diligently to remove the label "untouched" from the world's most extreme rock walls.

Cliffhanger: compared to David Lama, Sly Stallone is a complete amateur.

2004

Overall winner European Youth Cup; Youth World Champion

2006

With his first victory among adults, the 15-year-old David becomes the youngest World Cup winner in the history of climbing.

2007

During the European Championships in Birmingham David wins his second gold at a major competition.

2008

After winning the Combination World Cup, the overall rating of lead climbing and boulders, David increasingly directs his priorities towards alpine projects.

2012

First ascent of the legendary southeastern edge of the Cerro Torre by free climbing, which forsakes any technical equipment.

2013

First ascent of the central head wall of the Moose's Tooth in Alaska via the "Bird of Prey" route.

In January 2012, David was the first to free-climb the Cerro Torre in Patagonia, a milestone in alpinism. After the climb he had some fish he caught himself.

DINNER FOR ONE, GRILL PARTY FOR EVERYBODY.

[INTERVIEW]

SWEET OR SOUR?

From the gut, more like sour. But my memories of the chocolate shop El Chalten in Patagonia have me thinking again about this decision.

WHAT WAS YOUR BIGGEST NUTRITIONAL FAUX PAS BEFORE OR DURING A COMPETITION?

That was in 2009, during the World Championship in China. The organizers had arranged something for us athletes at a restaurant. Unfortunately, this restaurant wasn't so dedicated to hygiene. Some sixty athletes spent the following day in the bathroom, myself included.

TRY TO COMPARE YOUR SPORT TO A DISH. WHAT COMES TO MIND?

Uhm. No climbing tour is like the next, so it would be comparable to a menu consisting of dishes I don't know. The uncertainty before biting into an unfamiliar ingredient would be comparable to climbing in new regions during a first ascent.

WHAT ARE THE EVENINGS AND THE MORNINGS BEFORE A CLIMBING TOUR LIKE? WHAT'S ON YOUR PLATE AND IN YOUR GLASS?

For me it is more important to prepare myself mentally. I go through everything, check my plan, and get ready for the challenge.

HOW DO YOU CELEBRATE A SUCCESSFUL ALPINE ACHIEVEMENT?

With my friends and with a grill party.

IS THERE A RESTAURANT OR A SPECIAL PLACE WHERE YOU WOULD TAKE YOUR GIRLFRIEND OR WIFE FOR DINNER?

Schöneck restaurant in South Tirol. The only one missing is the woman.

WHICH THREE (LIVING OR HISTORIC) PEOPLE SIT AT THE TABLE OF YOUR PERFECT DINNER?

Doug Scott, Chris Bonington, and Mick Fowler. Three mountaineer legends from Britain. Their stories about adventures on the big mountains of the world would not fit into a single evening. But I would like to take care of the cooking myself; I don't trust the Brits that much in this matter (grins).

A VIEW INTO THE CRYSTAL BALL: WHAT COMES AFTER YOUR CAREER - MORE SIXPACK ABS OR SIX PACKS WITH BACON WRAP?

Generally I don't watch my nutrition that much. I love to eat and if it is good I can barely control myself. But I would definitely be physically active to compensate for it.

THE LONG WAY TO THE TOP

ENJOYMENT IN THE SEASONING.

Seasoning is the secret of successful dishes. Not even the most tender steak or the freshest fish can make up for a mistaken reach for salt and pepper. "There is nothing worse than dullness for the palate," says Roland Trettl. "You should season while preparing a dish—that is, in the pan or the pot. This allows for the taste to develop and bind." If you season a dish after cooking not much of it will be absorbed.

TROUT

WITH TWO KINDS OF APPLE

40 MINUTES

SCALE 5

INGREDIENTS:
- parsley
- 2 apples (Golden Delicious)
- 2 garlic cloves
- salt
- olive oil
- 4 trout (approx. 400 g [14 oz])
- 20 small potatoes
- 1 TBSP lemon juice
- 10 radishes
- 2 TBSP chopped chives
- butter
- pepper

DIP:
- 1 TBSP chives
- 4 TBSP yoghurt
- 4 TBSP low-fat curd
- lime zests
- 1 tsp tarragon
- olive oil
- salt

One last check of the list of ingredients by master chef Roland Trettl before his guest of honor arrives. The basics are there, but not one hint of amounts or weights or volumes, required spices, or, generally speaking, any indication as to preparation time.

Roland doesn't have to wonder for a long time. David Lama has stealthily approached the countertop and gazes at the ingredients with a kind of look that the rock walls of Europe, Asia and the rest of the world only know too well: determination.

David reaches for the baking paper and cuts two equal-sized sheets and places them on the countertop. His eyes fixate on Roland who knows right away: this man knows what he's doing.

David Lama picks the parsley leaves while Roland chops them up and gestures towards the apples: "How small do you want it?" "Into eighths," he replies. "And leave the skin on." Short and precise indications, that's the way the Ikarus chef likes it—he does so every day in his kitchen.

The garlic cloves are mashed and mixed with salt and parsley and both baking paper sheets are lightly brushed with olive oil and coated with some garlic mix. The trout are placed on top of it before Roland makes precise cuts into their skin.

Then the trout are marinated once again with oil, garlic mix, and lemon juice, and the apple slices are placed on top of them. "Do you cook a lot?," asks Roland while David Lama is struggling with the trout and baking paper, because the trout are now wrapped in it: "I cook regularly only during expeditions. But there's no gourmet food there."

The oven has been preheated to 160 degrees (325°F). "I'd say 15 minutes," Roland suggests. But David protests: "That's not sufficient, no way, 20 at least!" "We'll see," Roland insists, and the wrapped trout (David lovingly calls them "calzone") are placed on a baking tray and disappear inside the oven. While the fish is simmering both of them take care of the precooked potatoes and peel them. Then the radishes are quartered and some chives are chopped.

"So, you like to fish," the master chef teases his counterpart for some lively discussion. "I'd die of boredom!" "Not a chance " replies David. "Angling is even more exciting than climbing. You never know what's coming; you have to read the water, think like a fish, observe the current. You need a lot of intuition—just as with cooking."

The question of all questions and always relevant, even in the kitchen: Who is right?

1:0 for the guest ...

Now it's the turn of the side dish. Roland melts small cubes of butter in the pan and adds the potatoes, radishes, and chives. The mix is seasoned vigorously with salt and pepper and fried until it is nicely golden.

A "Chief, the 15 minutes are over" interrupts the scene. The moment of truth has arrived and the "calzone" are carefully opened. "No way! It really needs a few more minutes," shouts Roland. He carefully avoids David Lama's "I told you so" grin.

Now it is the dip's turn. The chives are finely chopped and mixed with yogurt and low-fat curd. Roland adds some lime zest and tarragon to the dip. Finally, a dash of olive oil and salt are mixed in as well.

Meanwhile, the radishes have turned a transparent light pink, indicating they are done. The roasted trout is removed from the oven and carefully filleted, the side dish is placed on plates, and the dip in the bowl is served.

The executive chef is floored. "Next year I shouldn't bring in guest cooks, but athletes such as yourself," he raves while David Lama eats the trout with Buddhist-syle serenity. "Sure, and the fish will be nice and done, too," David laughs.

And now the score is 2:0.

BMX RACER

SPAIN
RESIDENCE: MADRID

SERGIO LAYOS

COMET ON WHEELS.

NAME: Sergio Layos

NICKNAME: Hanson

BIRTHDAY: July 13, 1985

HEIGHT: 1.68 m (5' 5")

WEIGHT: 65 kg (143 lbs)

DISCIPLINE: BMX street, BMX dirt

HOBBY: surfing

TWITTER: @SergioLayos

Usually, thirteen-year-olds get their heads turned. In the case of Sergio Layos it was somewhat different. He turned the heads of accomplished riders of the BMX scene when he won second place at the World Championship in Portugal. If you think about the fact that back then he had barely two years of experience on a bike and that there were almost no skate parks where he lived—not to mention sponsors—this is a pretty incredible story. Sergio Layos has been part of the international BMX scene since 1999, and he is among the top names. But the Spaniard doesn't draw his motivation from winning important contests: "People forget them after a few weeks anyway. The most exciting thing about my sport is making great videos, seeing cool locations all over the world, and doing the craziest stuff on a BMX."

2009

2. place Asian X-Games/Shanghai, China

2010

1. place Rebel Jam/Portimao, Portugal

2011

1. place Nike Pool Contest/UK
1. place Molletazo Contest/Spain
1. place Rebel Jam/Netherlands
Finalist RIDEuk Summer Sessions/Finland

2012

Finalist Simple Session/Tallinn, Estonia

"I HAVE NO DOUBT: IF I WOULDN'T DO BMX I WOULDN'T BE AS HAPPY AS I AM."

STINKING PASSION.

[INTERVIEW]

WHEN DOES YOUR DISCIPLINED ATHLETE'S HEART BECOME WEAK? WHAT DO YOU NEVER PICK UP WITH A FORK?

I am a vegetarian and I love cheese in all its varieties, even the stinking moldy cheese types. Artichokes I really can't stand at all.

WHAT WAS YOUR BIGGEST MISTAKE REGARDING NUTRITION BEFORE OR DURING A COMPETITION?

Once in the US I went to a waffle house just before a competition, one of the well-known fast food chains. I filled my stomach with all kinds of waffles and omelets. Riding BMX afterwards was pure hell.

WHAT ARE THE EVENINGS AND THE MORNINGS BEFORE YOUR COMPETITION LIKE? WHAT'S ON YOUR PLATE AND IN YOUR GLASS?

Leaving the waffle house aside, usually I eat something light for breakfast. Cornflakes for example, with freshly-squeezed orange juice. The day before I eat pasta—it provides power.

HOW DO YOU CELEBRATE A SUCCESSFUL COMPETITION?

In case I win a really important title—for example at the X-Games—I'll make a huge firewood oven pizza for all of my buddies.

YOUR PERSONAL RESTAURANT SUGGESTION?

There's an inside tip in Madrid, far away from the well-known streets. The place is called "La Cúpula"; that's where they make the best pizzas on earth.

YOU HAVE ONE LAST MEAL. WHAT WOULD YOU ORDER?

"Potaje"—a typical Spanish dish my grandmother used to prepare. And since I have a free wish, she should be the one preparing it.

WHO ARE THE THREE PEOPLE SITTING AT THE TABLE OF YOUR PERFECT DINNER?

My older brother, no question. Then it would be Guiri, my best friend who introduced me to BMX racing back then. And Joe Rich, he's something like a mentor to me—a really cool guy and a real BMX legend.

THE LONG WAY TO THE TOP

A GOOD EGG NEEDS TIME.

How do you boil the perfect egg? This question has led to many agitated discussions at the breakfast table. However, the master chef should know, and here is the answer: "Heat the egg placed in a container with cold water at 65 degrees (150°F) for one hour inside the oven," says Roland Trettl. Why is the long wait worth it? Egg white and yolk acquire the same texture, so the egg has the same softness inside and out.

GAZPACHO

60 MINUTES

SCALE 4

INGREDIENTS:
- 2 eggs
- 2 cucumbers
- 4 bell peppers (2 red, 2 yellow)
- 200 g (7 oz) cherry tomatoes
- 1 red onion
- 4 slices of toasted bread (without crust)
- 10 basil leaves
- salt, chili powder
- about 20 g (¾ oz) rice vinegar or red wine vinegar
- 1 shallot
- 100 g (3 1/3 oz) olive oil
- 8 anchovy fillets
- 1 garlic clove

One hour before Sergio Layos makes the first move in the kitchen of Hangar-7 Roland Trettl has started to work on the gazpacho—a traditional cold Spanish vegetable soup.

What has taken so long? He has boiled two eggs. This can be a real science, as many hobby cooks can attest to But few treat this matter as methodically as the chef of Ikarus—see "The long way to the top."

"You really didn't have to do this," Sergio is moved when he hears about the preparations performed by Roland after he arrives. "I usually just hardboil the eggs. That tastes good, too."

Whether perfectionist or pragmatist— the first step towards a gazpacho has been taken, so Sergio and Roland deal with the next one. While cutting and chopping the cucumbers, bell pepper, and cherry tomatoes (half of it into large and half of it into small cubes) and onion (only large pieces), the blades of the knives become red hot.

"You know, I once ran a restaurant myself" ...

... recounts Sergio. "My mother, my brother, and I had a restaurant in my hometown of Majadahonda very close to Madrid. But over time it was simply too stressful, so a few years ago we sold it with some regret."

The coarse pieces of bell pepper, cucumber, tomato, and onion are put in a deep bowl together with a few large pieces of toast, the mashed garlic, and basil leaves. It is seasoned with salt and chili powder, then Roland adds a mix of 250 g (8½ oz) of water and 20 g (¾ oz) of vinegar.

"Now the bowl should be placed outside in the sun for two hours so the taste can develop optimally," says Roland, and Sergio adds: "In Spain you can do that. But look at this weather," gesturing towards the window with a low cloud cover outside. "I think we just keep going."

Roland pours the contents of the bowl into the blender and turns it on, tastes

it, and seasons some more. Then he strains the soup through a sieve back into the bowl.

The small pieces of cucumber, bell pepper, and tomato are placed on a plate, salted, and seasoned with chili powder. Sergio also cuts a few rings from shallots and Roland adds a dash of vinegar and olive oil.

The fact that Roland has used Japanese rice vinegar almost knocks Sergio out of his socks: "Rice vinegar?!" "You will see how good it tastes," laughs Roland. "I used to work in Mayorca for a few years and I also made gazpacho. Not one Spaniard ever complained." He adds: "If you don't have rice vinegar handy you can use red wine vinegar instead."

While Sergio shakes his head incredulously, the Ikarus chef prepares the gazpacho. First the small pieces of vegetables are put in the soup bowl. Roland then cuts up two anchovy fillets over each portion, as well as an egg, and then adds the soup.

They sit down to eat at a table in the warehouse of Hangar-7, down-to-earth style. There's a good reason for the master chef, as the born Italian wants to have his very personal rematch against the Spaniard regarding the lost European Championship of 2012: table football. "Okay, no problem," laughs Sergio, "but first let's eat something, I'm starving."

Sergio thoughtfully tastes the first spoon of gazpacho, leaves it on his tongue for a long time, and makes big eyes: "Hey, this rice vinegar is really great!" Roland smiles triumphantly: "I told you so."

"Japanese vinegar with gazpacho ... if I told my mom at home she would have a heart attack."

Successful return game: Roland kicks Sergio out of the warehouse, 3:0.

ALPINE SKIER

NORWAY
RESIDENCE: INNSBRUCK, AUSTRIA

AKSEL LUND SVINDAL

TAKE IT ALL. BUT TAKE IT EASY.

NAME: Aksel Lund Svindal

BIRTHDAY: December 26, 1982

HEIGHT: 1.89 m (6' 2")

WEIGHT: 98 kg (216)

DISCIPLINE: downhill, Super G, giant slalom, super combined

HOBBIES: windsurfing, motocross

WEBSITE: www.aksellundsvindal.com

Golden boy and ski racer—what a match this can be has been shown to the world by Aksel Lund Svindal now for over a decade, and quite successfully so. Two overall World Cup victories, five gold medals at World Cups, and one Olympic gold medal are only the absolute highlights of an incredible career that began at age three on the home hill of his birthplace, Lørenskog.

Aksel had to get up from the ground, both in sports and privately. At age eight he lost his mom (whose maiden name Lund he proudly bears today) in a tragic way. Perhaps this blow allowed him to approach dealing with the daily challenges of the sport and of life itself in a more relaxed way. Aksel Lund Svindal knows that you have to work hard for your achievements, and he knows how to celebrate them.

2007

Winner Overall World Cup; 1. place giant slalom World Cup; 1. place Combined World Cup; downhill World Cup-gold; giant slalom World Cup-gold

2009

Winner Overall World Cup; 1. place Super-G-World Cup; World Cup-gold Super Combination; World Cup-bronze Super-G

2010

Olympia-Gold Super-G; Olympia-silver downhill; Olympia-bronze giant slalom

2011

World Cup-Gold super combination

2012

1. place Super-G-World Cup

2013

1. place downhill World Cup; 1. place Super-G World Cup; World Cup-Gold downhill; World Cup-Bronze Super-G

Mister speed: Kitzbühel is Aksel's favorite race. "Towards the finish it's like you are driving into a cave full of people."

DAD AS TEACHER OF INDULGENCE.

[INTERVIEW]

TRY TO COMPARE YOUR SPORT TO A DISH. WHAT COMES TO MIND?

I'd think perhaps a huge steak full of protein and a wholesome salad as a side dish would be appropriate.

WHAT WAS YOUR BIGGEST FAUX PAS REGARDING NUTRITION BEFORE A COMPETITION?

That happened at my first downhill race in Kitzbühel; the biggest mistake was not to have eaten anything. For two reasons, actually: during the race I was extremely weak, and during the evening I filled up with Indian food—something I very much regretted the next twenty-four hours.

HOW DO YOU CELEBRATE A SUCCESSFUL RACE?

The best part is that once you are done with all the hubbub, the award ceremony, media sessions, and all, in the evening you can be around the people who took part in the victory. It doesn't matter what is being eaten or drank, the atmosphere is what matters.

AT THE TABLE WITH FAMILY AND FRIENDS: ARE YOU THE FIRST ONE TO FINISH YOUR PLATE OR DO YOU ENJOY EVERY BITE?

When I am on tour with my teammates I am always the last one. Then I think: "Wow, you are a slow eater." But when I sit with my dad at home ... the man redefines the term "connoisseur."

YOU WAKE UP IN THE MIDDLE OF THE NIGHT WITH THE MUNCHIES. WHAT HAS TO BE IN YOUR FRIDGE?

As I spent most of my time in hotel rooms I don't have my own fridge, but I always need a glass of water next to my bed. And there's always some sort of snack or something sweet, just in case.

WHAT WAS IT YOU COULDN'T STAND AS A CHILD? AND DO YOU LIKE IT TODAY?

Olives—and yes, today, I rather like them.

YOU HAVE ONE LAST MEAL. WHAT WOULD YOU ORDER?

I would invite all of my friends to a barbecue. We would stand around the grill, watching the fire and having a beer, chatting, and enjoying a really good time.

THE LONG WAY TO THE TOP

BREAST OR LEG?

This all-important question was asked by the French comedian Louis de Funès in his 1970s film classic. The answer comes forty years later from Roland Trettl. "When I cook chicken I only use the legs." Because of their streaked meat—similar to the neck in the case of pork—the legs are particularly juicy and tasty. Trettl: "Chicken breast is bound to turn out dry."

GREEN THAI CURRY

40 MINUTES

SCALE 5

INGREDIENTS:

4 chicken legs
5 kaffir limes*
1 tsp chopped ginger
1 eggplant
1 bunch green asparagus
2 shallots
2 bell peppers (red and yellow)
1 green chili pod
3 TBSP green curry paste*
200 g (6¾ oz) coconut milk*
2 TBSP palm sugar* or cane sugar
fish sauce*
250 g (8¾ oz) organic rice
1 bunch of cilantro
1/2 lime

*The ingredients marked with a * can be purchased in Asian food stores.*

Does a man who races down a slope at 150 kph (93 mph) know the word "fear"? And if so, can he pronounce it without stumbling?

Roland Trettl is rather surprised when Aksel Lund Svindal tells him he's pretty afraid of the joint cooking session at Ikarus. "You race down the hill in Wengen or Kitzbühel without batting an eye, and you are afraid of the kitchen? You can't be serious!"

But Aksel's reply makes sense: "If you don't have respect for things that are new to you, you won't get far in life." "Respect!," Trettl nods. "That's what I call some philosophy."

And Svindal's philosophy for the kitchen? The cool Norwegian laughs:

"Better don't touch anything."

"I get around so much I can't do any cooking, and when I have some time with my girlfriend she usually takes care of it."

His relationship with professional colleague Julia Mancuso also provided the idea for his current favorite dish. "Julia lives on Maui in her spare time ...," Aksel starts out—and right away Roland cuts him off: "Maui? No wonder you fall in love. With the food!"

For the green Thai curry, the master chef has previously removed the marrow from the chicken legs but left the skin intact. Both of them cut the legs into pieces of several centimeters (one inch).

Then the lime leaves are chopped. "Please, as finely as possible. Can you do that?," asks Roland. But the powerhouse apparently has some difficulty with the finishing work. "You can tell that in the end the concentration went downhill," Trettl laughs during the final inspection.

A finger-sized piece of ginger is also chopped into fine cubes. Together with the lime leaves they are put in a bowl and set aside.

Now the two of them get to work on the eggplant, asparagus, shallots, bell peppers, and chili, cutting them into large pieces. "But be careful, I don't like it too spicy," Aksel tells the master chef, who takes a small bite of the chili and immediately gets misty-eyed: "Okay, we'd better leave out the chili."

They are done with the preparations —next stop, the stove. The cook heats about 3 TBSP of curry paste in a wok and adds coconut milk and some water to it. "The important thing now is to check the spiciness," Trettl says. "This here is the foundation for the dish. Later it will lose some spiciness due to the vegetables, but at any rate it shouldn't be too hot right now."

The foundation is boiled with the lime leaves and some palm sugar. Then the previously prepared vegetables and the meat are put in the pan. Add water, the remaining coconut milk, and a dash of fish sauce so that the contents is barely covered and allow to simmer.

While the meat and vegetables are boiling it is convenient to prepare the rice. Aksel and Roland utilize a rice cooker for practical reasons: "Simply because it's faster." But when selecting the type of rice, the master chef is much more picky. "I suggest organic rice. It's simply tastier because the aroma stays in the grain." "And you can't overcook it like white rice," Aksel adds. Apparently, this is a long-suffering man speaking ...

Now they get back to dealing with the wok. Once the meat and vegetables are done and the sauce is thick and creamy and some cilantro has been added the final sampling can be performed. "Spiciness is fine," says Roland. "Perhaps some more salt?" "No, it's fine the way it is. But do you have some lime? It would add freshness to the taste." And just like that Roland squeezes out half a lime over the wok. "We shouldn't tell any Thai about this," he laughs. "They don't do this, no way. But with respect to the taste, you are totally correct— and we're in Salzburg, after all, not Bangkok."

The cook orders freshly-made iced tea to accompany the dish. Then he serves the dish in a bowl: first the rice, then the Thai curry, and finally some cilantro on top of it. But Trettl is still not entirely satisfied: "Thai food simply never looks too attractive when it's on the plate."

The naked truth: Thai dishes are not cooked in a wok and Thai people don't eat with chopsticks! Trettl: 'Only we Europeans believe that."

"That depends on how you define attractiveness," replies Aksel.

"In my opinion, if it tastes great it is attractive."

And regarding this matter the two are of the same opinion after tasting the first bite: the Thai curry could compete at any beauty contest.

Coming home for the Christmas goose: during summer Aksel lives on Maui, and during the season in South Tirol. "Unfortunately I don't get to Norway that often, but Christmas is on the agenda every year."

SKI MOUNTAINEER

AUSTRIA
RESIDENCE: KITZBÜHEL

AXEL NAGLICH

ARCHITECT OF FEAR.

NAME: Axel Naglich

BIRTHDAY: February 28, 1968

HEIGHT: 1.74 m (5' 7")

WEIGHT: 73 kg (161 lbs)

PROFESSION: architect

HOBBIES: skiing, triathlon, climbing, delta-flying, paragliding

Who is Axel Naglich? That's not easy to answer, as there are very few of his kind on this planet. Axel Naglich is a mountaineer, ice climber, and extreme skier all in one. He constantly searches for new challenges. He climbs untouched mountain walls and then races down via steep and out-of-the-way slopes. He was in the Himalayas, skied down the highest mountain in Europe, traveled through South America for many years, and left his turns at the Damavand in Iran. As a "sideline" Axel Naglich also runs an architectural firm. This is a contradiction on the surface only. Just like his buildings, his tours require precise planning. The smallest error can be too much.

"When it turns out okay you are a hero, if it goes bad you're dead."

DESTINATIONS SO FAR & FIRST DESCENTS:

Alpes, Himalaya, Mount St. Elias (Alaska), Elbrus (Russia), Damavand (Iran), Mount Cook (New Zealand)

RACES:

24 hours of Aspen: 5 participations, 3 victories (1993, 1996, and 1997), participation at international ski cross competitions for over 10 years, Red Bull Snowthrill in Chamonix, France: participation in 1998 and 1999, X-Games: two participations, Ironman: three participations in Austria

MOUNT ST. ELIAS

"If you want to do something big you have to give up something big. If you want to achieve something really great you have to risk even more."
Axel Naglich

CHECK OUT: www.mountstelias.com

UP THE MOUNTAIN WITH A LOAD OF EGGS.

[INTERVIEW]

COOKING IS ...

... a nice thing—I can be really enthusiastic about the results. In my case, there is not much chance of success due to a lack of skills! I rather rely on professionals such as Roland and my wife, who is definitely better at it than I am.

TRY TO COMPARE YOUR SPORT TO A DISH. WHAT COMES TO MIND?

Salzburger Nockerl (gnocchi). You need some basic know-how for the ingredients and patience for the preparation, and in the end the whole thing can still fall apart because of a small error.

WHICH CHARACTERISTIC UNITES A SUCCESSFUL MOUNTAINEER WITH A GOOD COOK?

Endurance and focusing on one specific thing that has particular appeal in its details. And then there is this indescribable joy when a project is successful.

WHAT DOES THE EVENING AND THE MORNING BEFORE A TOUR LOOK LIKE? WHAT'S ON YOUR PLATE AND IN YOUR GLASS?

Before you go on a mountain tour, it is important that you load up on carbohydrates. While on tour protein is important, so I eat a lot of eggs. But my basic motto is: whatever I eat beforehand I don't have to carry up the mountain (laughs).

A RESTAURANT OR A SPECIAL PLACE WHERE YOU WOULD TAKE A WOMAN OUT FOR DINNER?

That's a long list. Too long. I couldn't finish it during the rest of my life. Just in my hometown of Kitzbühel there are so many good places, and I really should take her out to Ikarus again one of these days.

THE TASTE OF YOUR CHILDHOOD?

Malt coffee, overripe pears, currant juice, cranberries, and Wiener schnitzel. The latter one was served only occasionally, as it was the typical Sunday dish at home, so it automatically became my favorite dish as a child.

BEER IN THE GARDEN OR A GLASS OF WINE AT THE BAR?

I don't like the taste of beer or wine. I can only drink alcohol when mixed with Red Bull until you can't taste the alcohol anymore. Whether it's the garden or the bar doesn't matter.

YOU HAVE ONE LAST MEAL. WHAT WOULD YOU ORDER?

An Austrian specialty: soured boiled rump with roasted potatoes and apple horseradish.

THE LONG WAY TO THE TOP

ICE-COLD AND HEATED.

The base for soup is the stock—an essential flavor carrier. Roland Trettl suggests using ice-cold water—mixed with ice cubes is best. The reason: "Due to the sudden chilling and reheating the nutrients of the ingredients can fully develop." The soup will be even more aromatic and taste better.

CREAMY CRAYFISH SOUP

50 MINUTES

SCALE 6

INGREDIENTS:

20 crayfish
170 g (6 oz) cherry tomatoes
130 g (4½ oz) carrots
300 g (10½ oz) fennel
120 g (4¼ oz) celery stalks
3 onions
1 garlic clove
olive oil
1 TBSP tomato paste
60 g (2 oz) butter
salt
chili powder
60 g (2 oz) white wine
60 g (2 oz) vermouth
50 g (1¾ oz) cognac
ice cubes
thyme
basil
tarragon
1/2 lemon
4 g (1/3 oz) whipped cream

Anticipation: a sample in between can't be bad.

"Rip off the head! Break up the belly, where the feet are located. And then slowly remove the meat." No, this is not a manual for icky and illegal activities. Rather, it's the guide for cleaning crayfish. Not entirely unimportant for Axel Naglich's favorite dish.

But somehow the extreme ski mountaineer and confessed anti-cook must have thought this was easier. Too bad when you only know the dish as it's served at a restaurant ...

"I should have asked for a Kaiserschmarrn," he curses while Roland looks with a keen eye at his hands: "And don't forget the pincers, there's meat in them, too."

After what seems like an eternity the procedure is finally over.

"To summit is nothing compared to this" ...

... teases the master chef. And the work with the creamy crayfish soup has just begun.

If you think the removed shells have done their deed you are mistaken. "They are an important flavor carrier," explains Trettl, who puts them in a plastic bag and pats it several times. Then its time to fling the blades. The cherry tomatoes are cut in half, same for the carrots—lengthwise and then into pieces. And then Axel and Roland chop fennel, celery, onion, and garlic.

All of this is put in a deep pan with the crayfish scale pieces and some olive oil and mixed well. After one minute tomato paste and butter are added and seasoned with salt and chili powder. Important: keep stirring while frying.

What do you eat when on tour to the Nanga Parbat or to Mount St. Elias? "Dry food from a can.

You feel like you're in a war.

But I've made a virtue out of necessity and developed a beef stroganoff with the manufacturer. It's actually quite passable."

"And what are the nutritional values of such food?," asks Roland Trettl with a slightly grossed-out expression. "You won't believe it, but it's got everything you need when you're up there."

The attention shifts from the boring food on the mountain back to the stove. And to the alcohol that comes into play now. After the contents of the pan has turned brown Roland adds white wine, vermouth, and cognac.

"Watch out!"—with a surprise attack with the Bunsen burner the Ikarus chef sets the dish ablaze. "If you're too queasy about having a large flame inside your own kitchen you can leave out this prodedure," grins Roland. Axel adds: "Although it is pretty spectacular ..." The matter is extinguished with 1 l (4¼ cups) of cold water and two handfuls of ice cubes (see "The long way to the top").

Now the contents of the pan simmers over low heat for thirty minutes. At about half the time, whipped cream and a twig of thyme are added. Furthermore, it is a good idea to sample and season if required.

While the stock simmers Axel has to once again reach for the knife, like it or not. Small cubed pieces of carrot, fennel, and celery are required. They are put in a deep pan and briefly fried in hot olive oil.

Now Roland pours the stock from one pan into the other through a sieve, so the pieces of shell won't get through. "Although I like it crunchy, in this case it wouldn't be too great," Axel comments from a safe distance.

His favorite dish is almost done. Almost! Because without the previously removed crayfish meat there's no deal. So in it goes, boiled up once more with some basil and tarragon, as well as the juice of half a lemon. Then it's time to set the table.

"I am really proud of myself," Axel laughs. "This is the best crayfish soup I have ever prepared."

BMX RACER

COLOMBIA
RESIDENCE: MEDELLÍN

MARIANA PAJÓN

MEDALS FROM MEDELLÍN.

NAME: Mariana Pajón

NICKNAME: Tata

BIRTHDAY: October 10, 1991

HEIGHT: 1.58 m (5' 2")

WEIGHT: 53 kg (117 lbs)

DISCIPLINE: BMX racing

HOBBIES: gymnastics, go-kart

WEBSITE: www.marianapajon.com.co

TWITTER: @marianapajon

Not really that beautiful, but pretty dangerous. You better not write this about a woman, but this isn't about the woman; rather, about her home: Medellín, the second-largest city of Colombia, has the image of a street dog. In the best of cases you just don't get close to it. This applies to the over two million residents: if you want to persevere here you have to fight. Mariana Pajón has fought since her early childhood. She didn't hesitate to apply her most dangerous weapon, either: the BMX. The born rider got her first national title at age five and her first international title at age ten. A decade later, Mariana climbed up Mount Olympus: Gold in London. If they call you "Queen of BMX" when you are this young you've made it. Out of Medellín and into the hearts of people. By the way, yes, Mariana Pajón is dangerous. And beautiful.

Mariana's philosophy is borrowed from Eleanor Roosevelt: "The future belongs to those who believe in the beauty of their dreams."

2008
WC-gold (Junior Women Cruiser)

2009
WC-gold (Junior Women Cruiser); WC-Gold (Junior Women)

2010
WC-gold (Elite Women Cruiser)

2011
WC-gold (Elite Woman) & World Championship-bronze (Elite Woman Time Trial); Pan-American Games-gold

2012
Olympia-gold (Women's BMX)

2013
WC-gold (Elite Woman BMX Time Trial)

Tough one: after a major crash Mariana Pajón has nine screws and two metal plates in her arm.

A BURGER WITH THE GOLDEN ONE.

[INTERVIEW]

WHEN DOES YOUR DISCIPLINED ATHLETE'S HEART BECOME WEAK?

Popcorn, chocolate ice cream, and banana splits. I can't miss these in my nutrition. I eat whatever I feel like anyway. My attitude towards food: If I don't feel great I can't perform too well.

AND WHAT DO YOU NEVER PICK UP WITH A FORK?

I can't stand fish, with one exception: tuna.

WHAT WAS YOUR GREATEST MISTAKE REGARDING NUTRITION BEFORE OR DURING A COMPETITION?

The body needs too much energy to digest beans or red meat right before a competition. I've tried it and I can confirm it (laughs).

HOW DO YOU CELEBRATE A SUCCESSFUL COMPETITION?

After winning Olympia the first thing I did was go to McDonald's. After a full month I was tired of noodles and all I wanted was a huge burger with french fries.

WHAT CAN BE FOUND IN YOUR FREEZER?

Meat, chicken, pizza, vegetables, mozzarella sticks, ice cream, and a couple of frozen Red Bull cans.

YOUR PERSONAL RESTAURANT SUGGESTION?

"San Carbon" in my hometown of Medellín. They have some amazing Mexican food. And then there's a fast food chain in South America called "Crepes & Waffles." If you are ever there, don't miss it!

YOU HAVE ONE LAST MEAL. WHAT DO YOU ORDER?

A coffee smoothie with caramel, a huge pepperoni pizza, and a gigantic banana split.

AT THE TABLE WITH FAMILY AND FRIENDS: ARE YOU THE FIRST ONE TO FINISH OR DO YOU ENJOY EVERY SINGLE BITE?

I am the first one to finish and enjoy every single bite of the dessert.

WHICH THREE (STILL LIVING OR HISTORIC) PERSONS ARE SITTING AT THE TABLE OF YOUR PERFECT DINNER?

Nelson Mandela, Haile Gebrselassie, and Ayrton Senna. They are my total heroes; it would be fantastic to share stories and experiences with them.

THE LONG WAY TO THE TOP

POTATOLOGY: SERIOUS SCIENCE.

Throw into the water and wait? Preparing potatoes is a lot more than that. Trettl: "Never peel the potatoes before boiling them. And put them into the water only when it is already boiling!" Otherwise they lose too many vitamins. A good alternative to boiling is steaming: the vitamins and aromatic compounds are better preserved due to lower heat.

By the way: is it true that there are poisons being released when reheating potatoes? "Total baloney," says Trettl. "But one thing's for sure: the taste won't get any better with reheating."

AJIACO CON POLLO

60 MINUTES

SCALE 3

INGREDIENTS:

150 g (51/3 oz) potatoes (e.g., Bellarosa)
150 g (51/3 oz) potatoes (waxy)
150 g (51/3 oz) potatoes (mealy)
1 chicken
50 g (1¾ oz) olive oil
2 onions
2 garlic cloves
2 tomatoes (chopped finely)
salt
1 sprig of thyme
10 pieces of baby corn cob
150 g (5 oz) cream
250 g (1 cup) rice
3 tsp capers
2 avocados
1 l (4¼ cups) water or poultry stock

Cooking like grandma in Colombia? This sounds like fun in the kitchen. But it also sounds like work, as there are several ingredients for Mariana Pajón's favorite dish—a traditional Colombian chicken stew—which are not easy to come by in Europe.

For starters, there's the potatoes: the most important ingredient of the dish apart from the chicken. Three different varieties are required—all of them with particular cooking characteristics so that the Ajiaco turns out really well. "These potatoes can't be found around here," declares Roland Trettl. "But fortunately there are comparable European varieties that can be used."

The chef of Ikarus suggests the following: a red potato with yellow pulp, such as the "Laura" or "Bellarosa" varieties. Fairly small and hard-boiling potatoes—Roland uses noble "La Ratte," but another alternative are "Bamberg Hörnchen." And finally, the typical oven potato—large and starchy.

The issue of spices also caused some concern before Mariana's visit. "Guasca" ("potato weed") provides its typical taste to the dish but is hard to come by. "Hence," according to Trettl, "we can take it easy and use thyme. Its taste is quite similar."

With these preparations the stage is set for a successful cooking session. Time for the main actress to take the stage. Wherever Mariana Pajón is

Under the skin: Mariana Pajón's triumph in London remains unforgotten. Tattoos on her forearms take care of this, too.

going, Olympia is always with her. She had the famous five rings tattooed on her left forearm: the right one says "Beyond Gold." And she brought along something else to Hangar-7: the golden one from London.

"Let's have a look," says Roland, rather excitedly. "I never had this much real gold in my hand." His personal medal count is now complete. After Vavra Hradilek's silver and Olga Kharlan's bronze (see previously) the executive chef of Ikarus has now cooked through all of the colors.

However, the Ajiaco is not done yet by a long shot. "Okay, let's get moving," Mariana suggests. While the two of them start peeling the mountain of potatoes and cut them into small pieces, two of Roland's industrious cooks lend a hand cutting the chicken breast into 4 cm (1½") pieces and add salt. Then the wings and legs are put into a deep pan with hot olive oil together with the chopped onions and garlic.

"If the onions are nice and crusty you can add the potatoes and tomatoes right away," says Roland. "Then you need to season well with salt so it won't taste dull under any circumstance."

After some five minutes, during which the chicken is fried pretty nicely, 1 l (4¼ cups) of water—or even better, poultry stock—is added with the chopped thyme and the contents of the pan is left to lightly simmer over low heat.

Now the chicken breast pieces are added to the pan, but not the baby corn—which Roland has cut into even pieces—or the cream. "Now allow to boil for as long as before," says Roland, and Mariana adds: "The longer the stew is boiling the more the potatoes fall apart, which thickens it even more. Actually, only one of the potatoes falls apart; the other varieties are hard-boiling."

Roland can't suppress a smile: "You've learned quite a lot from your grandma." "It would be great if it were so," counters the BMX queen, "but this is only theoretical knowledge. Grandma always tries to convince me to cook but I simply can't do it."

No worries, that's what the cooking professional is here for. And he is getting ready to dress the dish. He has boiled rice which is put in a bowl together with capers and pieces of avocado. The finished Ajiaco in the pan is then poured over it.

"This looks pretty awesome," says Mariana, who can hardly contain her excitement and who negotiates a small sample.

"Tastes like grandma's!"

Roland couldn't be happier: "For a cook there's no better compliment!"

BMX & MOUNTAIN BIKE RACER

CZECH REPUBLIC,
RESIDENCE: PRAGUE

MICHAL PROKOP

THE KING PREFERS TO WIN.

NAME: Michal Prokop

NICKNAME: Frky

BIRTHDAY: April 1, 1981

HEIGHT: 1.80 m (5' 9")

WEIGHT: 85 kg (187 lbs)

DISCIPLINE: BMX racing, mountainbike 4-cross

HOBBIES: enduro, street racing, skiing, cars

WEBSITE: www.prokoplive.com

TWITTER: @MichalProkop12

The "King of Czech Cycling" is the most important award for Czech riders, and for forty years it went exclusively to street riders—until Michal Prokop showed up with his fat tires. The joker—born in Prague—is a jack-of-all-trades and rides the spectacular mountainbike 4-cross as successfully as the demanding BMX tracks. The king's accolades: Prokop is a four-time World Champion, three-time European Champion, and two-time World Cup winner.

"My strengths? Speed and versatility!"

THE BIGGEST VICTORIES:

4 x World Champion – MTB-4 Cross
3 x European Champion – MTB-4 Cross
Winner of the Red Bull Pump Riders

Muscles and music: when Michal Prokop isn't sitting on his bike he's training at the gym. Trance comes through his headphones at full volume.

THE SOLDIER AND THE KING.

One of them is a daring pilot, the other a skilled BMX racer. One is tall as a tree, the other is short and muscular. One is calm and concentrated while the other is extroverted and always in a good mood. Despite the many differences between them, it's not only a common language why the two get along so well. The two Czech friends are united by the urge to redefine the boundaries of what is doable, something which can't be learned. Each one on his own with his sport, but sharing the success.

AEROBATIC PILOT

CZECH REPUBLIC
RESIDENCE: PARDUBICE

MARTIN SONKA

FROM AIR FORCE TO AIR RACE.

NAME: Martin Sonka

BIRTHDAY: March 26, 1978

HEIGHT: 1.89 m (6' 2")

WEIGHT: 90 kg (198 lbs)

HOBBIES: motorcycle, planes, flying

WEBSITE: www.martin-sonka.cz

FACEBOOK: www.facebook.com/MartinSonka

Martin Sonka caught air race fever from TV. The Czech Air Force pilot was commenting a race as an expert for the local broadcast company and the next season he was at the start. As the second-youngest pilot who has ever flown at an air race, Martin Sonka combines the elegant style of flying and capacity for quick learning of Red Bull Air Race legends Paul Bonhomme and Hannes Arch, and is therefore one of the hottest future aces of the "Formula 1 of the air."

2006

3. place Czech Championships (category: unlimited)

2007

2. place Czech Championships (category: unlimited)

2008

3. place World Aerobatic Cup (category: unlimited)

2009

5. place World Air Games (category: unlimited)

2010

14. place Red Bull Air Race World Championships

2011

2. place Freestyle World Championships

"I simply want to enjoy flying, meet cool people and, of course, be the best in the world."

NO DISH WITHOUT A BONE.

[INTERVIEW]

WHAT MAKES YOUR DISCIPLINED ATHLETE'S HEART BECOME WEAK? WHAT DO YOU NEVER PICK UP WITH A FORK?

Michal: I like everything except for red meat. Particularly Italian and Mexican food—and chickenburgers, of course!

Martin: Meat always has to be on my plate. If there isn't some bone sticking out of it, it's not really food to me (laughs).

WHAT WAS YOUR BIGGEST FAUX PAS REGARDING NUTRITION BEFORE OR DURING A COMPETITION?

Michal: When I was young I just ate anything. No wonder I was totally exhausted after two rounds.

Martin: Don't act as if you are watching your nutrition these days!

Michal: What do you know, anyway? (laughs). I definitely don't eat hot dogs before a race.

WHAT ARE THE EVENINGS AND MORNINGS BEFORE A COMPETITION LIKE? WHAT'S ON YOUR PLATE AND IN YOUR GLASS?

Martin: When I fly in the afternoon I always eat three eggs in the morning. Nothing afterwards, as I have to be careful so that food doesn't come up again while I am inside the plane.

Michal: The 4-cross races are all during summer, so for me it's particularly important to drink enough liquid.

HOW DO YOU CELEBRATE A SUCCESSFUL COMPETITION?

Michal: Only with beer, but quite a lot of it.

Martin: Same here. And with Vodka Bull.

ANY RESTAURANT OR A SPECIAL PLACE WHERE YOU WOULD LIKE TO DINE?

Michal: When I am in the US I always try to get to Key West, Florida, for a few days. A spectacular place with a huge number of great restaurants and bars.

Martin: There are so many exciting and exotic places on earth I'd like to get to know culinary-wise. Nevertheless, I believe in the saying the best place is at home.

YOU HAVE ONE LAST MEAL. WHAT WOULD YOU ORDER?

Martin: A huge steak with french fries.

Michal: How about chicken fajitas? Sounds like a fitting last meal.

THE LONG WAY TO THE TOP

WELL DONE IS NOT A COMPLIMENT ...

... at least not for a good piece of meat. Whoever wants to thoroughly cook meat can make a career at an American fast food chain starting with a capital M. But not Roland Trettl. "Meat should be cooked medium at the most. This keeps it juicy and preserves its aromas. Well done is a total no-go. Same for burgers. If you want a really good burger you shouldn't cook the inside entirely."

CHICKEN BURGER/ STEAK BURGER

40 MINUTES

SCALE 2

INGREDIENTS:

3 chicken legs and
200 g (7 oz) beef filet
1 onion
30 g (1 oz) olive oil
30 g (1 oz) butter
1 dash of curry powder, chili powder and paprika powder
12 slices of pork belly bacon
4 slices of cheese (e.g., Edam)
4 bread rolls
300 g (10½ oz) potato wedges
oil for frying
tomatoes in slices
5 leaves of iceberg lettuce

SAUCE:

1 onion
150 g (51/3 oz) pork belly bacon
olive oil
2 TBSP soy sauce
2 TBSP mustard
1 lime

If only Martin Sonka hadn't left the choice of dish to his friend. Michal Prokop asked for a nice large chicken burger. "Because I am very choosy with meat. I only like certain meats. Pork or beef I really don't like at all, but I do like bacon. It's strange, but it's been that way since my childhood."

Roland and Michal shape the burgers while Martin provides the lettuce.

"Oh man," laughs Sonka, who is staring at the prepared chicken meat. "Chicken burger! I should have known that it wouldn't turn out well with you." High time for Trettl to take an arbitrating role: "We could just improvise. Do you prefer beef filet for your burger?" The air race pilot happily accepts the offer. "Perfect, Roland! I love steak."

So catastrophe has been averted and the friendship is saved. It's a good thing the executive chef of Ikarus has his connections. One phone call is all it takes for a gorgeous beef steak to appear a few minutes later.

But it doesn't take away from the fact that general attention is once again directed towards the chicken, because it has to be shaped into ... burgers.

This is how it's done: pass the chicken meat through the meat grinder, then chop the onion into cubes and heat some olive oil until they are soft. Mix the ground meat with the onion and two slices of butter, add salt, and season with curry, paprika, and chili powder. The resulting mass can be shaped into burgers.

But before they are put into the pan one should prepare the sauce first. Briefly braise onion and bacon cubes in olive oil. "You can also add a dash of soy sauce," suggests Roland Trettl. "This adds a nice sour touch to the sauce." The fried bacon and onion cubes are mixed with mustard and the juice of half a lime, and that's it, the sauce is ready.

While Roland puts the chicken burger in one pan and the beef filet burger in another, frying them in hot olive oil, Michal and Martin stretch their necks to not miss a thing. "It's great to watch such an experienced cook up close," ponders Martin while witnessing the speed and precision of the Ikarus chef.

"Unfortunately there are not too many restaurants in the Czech Republic that are really top level," laments the air race pilot and, with all appropriate diplomacy, Roland has to agree with him: "I think there's currently only one that has a Michelin star."

"But our women are more beautiful," the athletes reply in unison. "It's just fair."

But not for Roland. He sentences the insolent guests to chop salad while he removes the fried meat from the pan to let it drip off and uses the still-hot olive oil to fry the bacon strips.

Now the burgers are loaded with a slice of cheese and placed in the oven heated at 200 degrees (400°F) until the cheese is golden and crispy. Trettl: "If you like your bread crispy as well, just add it too for one to two minutes." And because the frozen potato wedges are certainly not supposed to stay hard they are placed in the deep fryer. After the bath in hot oil the master chef adds a mix of curry, paprika, and chili powder.

Now all of the ingredients are done and the burgers can be built. The three of them diligently baste their burgers with the sauce: in the case of Michal and Roland, the burgers, and in the case of Martin the finely chopped filet steak. "Amazingly juicy and pink-colored meat," enthuses the pilot. Add some tomato slices, lettuce, and bacon, and the top lid.

"A real monster," Michal Prokop admires his towering piece of art.

"Too bad I'll have to destroy it now."

Bitefest: if you are going to eat a Michal Prokop chicken burger you better bring a strong jaw with you.

SKI JUMPER

AUSTRIA
RESIDENCE: FULPMES

GREGOR SCHLIERENZAUER

FLYING MAN WITH FORESIGHT.

NAME: Gregor Schlierenzauer

BIRTHDAY: January 7, 1990

HEIGHT: 1.80 m (5' 9")

DISCIPLINE: ski jumping, ski flying

HOBBIES: cooking, design

WEBSITE: www.gregorschlierenzauer.at

Higher, farther, more successful—and staying grounded. Gregor Schlierenzauer has managed to combine these factors. At twenty-three he is the most successful ski jumper in World Cup history. He also made history at the Four Hills Tournament: he was one of only two jumpers who defended their title at this important competition. He collects medals at the Olympic Games and World Cup Competitions like other people collect stamps. A sports wunderkind? Certainly. But one who, despite his tender age, already looks past the edge of the plate.

At the beginning of his major victories he discovered his passion for photography. Meanwhile, he has made a name for himself in this regard, as Schlierenzauer's exhibitions are appreciated in expert circles. The photographs document his routine, his travels, and allow glimpses behind the scenes of high performance sports. Perhaps this is even part of the secret of his refreshing and calm down-to-earth personality.

He is a bank whenever the issue is gold or precious metal: Schlierenzauer is something akin to a medal guarantee. His trophy shelf has ballooned to the size of a walk-in wardrobe. And all this at age twenty-three.

WITH OVER 50 WORLD CUP VICTORIES SCHLIERENZAUER IS THE MOST SUCCESSFUL SKI JUMPER OF ALL TIME!

OLYMPIC GAMES 2010

2 x bronze – single competition (long- and normal hill) Vancouver;
gold – team competition (long hill)

FOUR HILLS TOURNAMENT

2 x winner of the Four Hills Tournament (2011/2012 and 2012/2013)

WORLD CUP

2 x Overall World Cup winner (2008/2009 and 2012/2013)

WORLD CHAMPIONSHIPS

10 gold medals and 4 silver medals at world championships

An esthete, whether in sports or in life. His eye for perspective and special moments has made Schlierenzauer a highly regarded photographer.

GOURMET OF THE AIR.

[INTERVIEW]

WHICH FAMOUS SPORTSMAN/ SPORTSWOMAN WOULD YOU LIKE TO HAVE DINNER WITH?

Roger Federer. Somehow he is a real gentleman, he has charisma. He has been very successful, but he has stayed down-home.

THE TASTE OF YOUR CHILDHOOD IS ...

... lasagne! It has always been my favorite dish.

BEER IN THE GARDEN OR A GLASS OF WINE AT THE BAR?

I prefer beer with lemonade for grilling or a nice glass of red wine for dinner.

WHAT WAS THE CRAZIEST THING YOU EVER ATE?

Chicken testicles in Sardinia. Apparently it's a delicacy over there. Fortunately I wasn't aware of it at first, as I was so hungry. The waiter had served it as "compliments from the kitchen." When I found out what it was it was already in my stomach, but it wasn't too bad; a bit like chicken nuggets.

WHAT WAS IT YOU COULDN'T STAND AS A CHILD? AND DO YOU LIKE IT NOW?

Rice pudding, and I still hate it to this day. Simply disgusting!

AT THE TABLE WITH FAMILY AND FRIENDS: ARE YOU THE FIRST ONE TO FINISH OR DO YOU ENJOY EVERY SINGLE BITE?

I am a boarding school child, so I am more of the fast kind.

YOU ARE PLANNING A ROMANTIC DINNER FOR TWO: WHERE DOES IT TAKE PLACE?

Inside an old cottage in the Alps with a modern interior.

WHICH CHARACTERISTIC UNITES A SUCCESSFUL SKI JUMPER AND A GOOD COOK?

Goals. Preparation. Concentration. Improvisation. Enjoyment. Sweating ...

WHAT CAN BE FOUND IN YOUR FREEZER?

Vanilla ice cream and ice cubes for Red Bull.

WHERE DOES THE FUN STOP REGARDING FOOD?

With full plates that are returned.

COOKING IS ...

... relaxation. A piece of home. Energizing. To be in private and talk.

THE LONG WAY TO THE TOP

PORK: MORE TASTE, LESS FAT.

With the help of a paprika-salt mixture pork can be refined. Mix 500 g (17½ oz) of salt with 250 g (8¾ oz) of sugar and 125 g (4½ oz) of paprika powder and thoroughly massage into the meat. This causes fat to be removed from the meat and the taste to become more intense. After twenty minutes the salty crust is washed away and the meat is dabbed dry before processing it further.

ROASTED SUCKLING AND PORK BELLY

WITH POTATO-PARSLEY DUMPLINGS, RADISH-APPLE SALAD, AND MUSHROOMS.

180 MINUTES

SCALE 8

INGREDIENTS ROAST*:
5 celery stalks
5 carrots
4 onions
2 shoulders (from a suckling of about 5 kg [11 lbs])
125 g (4½ oz) paprika powder
600 g (21 oz) pork belly
200 g (6¾ oz) white wine
250 g (8¾ oz) sugar
salt and pepper

DUMPLINGS:
1 kg (2 lbs) potatoes, boiled and pressed
1 egg
1 egg yolk
20 g (¾ oz) parsley
4 TBSP potato starch
30 g (1 oz) butter
salt and pepper

RADISH-APPLE SALAD:
600 g (21 oz) radish
2 Granny Smith apples
40 g (1½ oz) pork belly
50 g (1¾ oz) white wine vinegar
50 g (1¾ oz) olive oil
salt and pepper

MUSHROOM SAUCE:
2 shallots
30 g (1 oz) butter
300 g (10½ oz) porcini
200 g (7 oz) chanterelle
1 TBSP parsley
100 g (3 1/3 oz) veal stock
balsamic vinegar
lemon juice

*ingredients for about 10 people.

Top score for rolling dumplings, handling the knife, and seasoning the ingredients. If Gregor should ever apply for another job after ski jumping and photography, a cook would be a promising choice.

The weight of flying objects is always a decisive factor, so ski jumpers are reported to be particularly prone to anorexia. "Just rumors" was the only comment the grinning Gregor Schlierenzauer uttered in the kitchen of Ikarus.

No additional words were necessary regarding this topic after a glance at Gregor's favorite dish: a roast, and a pork roast at that. Cooking is one of the high-flyer's favorite pastimes. The fact that this is not just a random comment becomes obvious when Gregor is tasked with chopping parsley later on. His handling of the knife appears to be proficient—almost professional—while he chops the herbs finely and with precision.

Meat starts with vegetables.

Trettl and Schlierenzauer chop the carrots and celery into large cubes and cut up an onion. On a baking dish they lay out the vegetables to form a bed for the meat.

To provide more taste to the suckling Trettl puts the pieces into a mixture of bell pepper and salt (see "The long way to the top"). After twenty minutes the mix is washed off again and the meat is dabbed dry.

Meanwhile, Schlierenzauer cuts the rind of the pork belly bacon some 5 mm (¼") deep in the shape of rhombs.

Now the pieces of meat are placed skin side up on the baking dish with the vegetables and cooked at 150 degrees (300°F) for 2 1/2 hours with convection.

Time for dumplings.

Trettl boils the potatoes in saltwater until they are soft, then peels them and puts them through the potato press. Meanwhile, Schlierenzauer melts butter in a pan until it is golden-brown. The liquid butter is then mixed with egg, egg yolk, and parsley. Then the green blend is mixed with the potatoes and the potato starch to form the dough for the dumplings. The two cooks shape small dumplings slightly larger than a table tennis ball and put them in gently simmering water. They are left for ten minutes in the open pot.

Mushrooms and salad.

For the mushroom sauce, Trettl fries the shallots in butter. Important: the pan has to be hot when the butter and onions are added to it. He then adds the finely chopped porcini and chanterelles. He lightly fries the mushrooms while stirring often and later adds the chopped parsley and the veal stock. The sauce is seasoned with a dash of vinegar and a dash of lemon juice.

Meanwhile, Gregor prepares the salad. He peels the radish and the apple. Using a square grater, he cuts them into longish strips and mixes thoroughly. Now Schlierenzauer roasts the bacon chopped into small cubes in a pan and deglazes with white wine vinegar. He places the crispy meat with the gravy over the salad. The composition is seasoned with salt and pepper—done!

The finish.

Once the pieces have taken on a golden-brown color Trettl removes the meat from the oven. He roasts the vegetables in a pan until they are light brown. Then he deglazes with white wine and some water, lets it simmer for twenty minutes, strains, and seasons the sauce. The meat is again placed in the oven for ten minutes on broil so the crust becomes nice and crispy.

As for food tasters Gregor Schlierenzauer has asked what must be the most honest critics imaginable to the chef's table of Ikarus' kitchen: his family. During the meal the first plans regarding Gregor's career as a chef are discussed by his brother, girlfriend, and parents. Not a bad idea. And likely the final nail in the coffin regarding the misconception about the eating habits of ski jumpers.

Seconds please! Just like any good cook, Gregor likes to eat abundantly.

RACE CAR DRIVER

BRAZIL
RESIDENCE: SÃO PAULO

DANIEL SERRA

STOCK CAR IN THE DNA.

NAME: Daniel Serra

NICKNAME: Serrinha

BIRTHDAY: February 24, 1984

HEIGHT: 1.68 m (5' 5")

WEIGHT: 65 kg (143 lbs)

DISCIPLINE: Stock Car Brazil

HOBBIES: triathlon, road race biking

TWITTER: @DanielSerra29

What do you do as the son of a triple stock car champion? Stupid question. Drive cars, of course—and if possible, faster than anyone else. At age fourteen with a go-kart, and at eighteen the switch to the European Formula Renault: Daniel Serra has always been in a hurry regarding his career.

Then came the downside in his life: no sponsors, no money, and back to Brazil. A setback? No. A challenge? Absolutely! Daniel Serra switched to stock car and into the footsteps of his dad Chico, former champion of Stock Car Brazil. Since 2007, Daniel has been in the cockpit for Red Bull Racing. Motto: sit low, stand high—on the podium.

Ironman: even off the road one should not mess with Daniel Serra. He regularly participates in the toughest triathlon events and is considered one of Brazil's most fit athletes.

2004

2. place Formula Renault 2.0 Brazil

2006

2. place Stock Car Light

2009

2. place Brazilian Endurance Championships

2010

3. place GT Brasil; 1. place Brazilian Endurance Championships

2011

2. place Brasilieiro de Marcas

2012

2. place Brazilian Endurance Championships

RACE CAR DRIVER

BRAZIL
RESIDENCE: SÃO PAULO

FELIPE FRAGA

LIVE YOUR DREAM.

NAME: Felipe Fraga

BIRTHDAY: July 3, 1995

HEIGHT: 1.77 m (5' 8")

WEIGHT: 67 kg (148 lbs)

DISCIPLINE: Stock Car Brazil Light

HOBBIES: angling, water skiing

TWITTER: @TheFelipeFraga

Felipe, Brazil, motor sports. Wasn't there something ... right! A name and one goal: just like his idol Felipe Massa, Felipe Fraga also wants to make it into Formula 1. Just a dream like hundreds of thousands of other Brazilian kids? Not at all. Felipe Fraga is not only talented, he is a future promise.

As a seven-year-old he won his first regional kart title, and at age ten he was already the overall Brazilian Kart Champion. After a stopover in Europe as a pilot in Formula 2.0, Felipe has been racing for the Stock Car Brazil Light Series since 2013. In other words, he is winning. Just in his first three races he celebrated three victories, all from the pole position. This is a dominance that calls for more. All of this can lead to the formulation of high-flying goals: "One day I'll be driving for Red Bull Racing in the premier league."

2009

1. place Pan-American Kart;
1. place Brazilian Kart Cup;
The youngest pilot to qualify for the Petrobras Kart Selective

2010

1. place Petrobras Kart Selective
1. place Brazilian Kart Cup

2011

1. place Brazilian Super Kart Championship;
2. place Brazilian Kart Cup;
1. place Gatorz Challenge

2012

3. place Formula Renault 2.0 (1. race);
4. place Formula Renault 2.0 Alps (2. race)

SKY
Red Bull
racing

Every inch counts: exciting wheel-to-wheel duels make stock car one of the world's most spectacular motor sports series.

Unknown terrain: while visiting Austria Danie Serra and Felipe Fraga hotly compete on the snow kart track at Saalbach-Hinterglemm. The subsequent bonfire brings the two Brazilians back to operating temperature.

BEING CRAZY IS NOT A DISADVANTAGE.

[INTERVIEW]

WHAT MAKES YOUR DISCIPLINED ATHLETE'S HEART WEAK? WHAT DO YOU NEVER PICK UP WITH A FORK?

Daniel: I have a weakness for french fries. Who doesn't like them? However, what I don't like that much—sorry to say this, don't take it badly—are Austrian dumplings. Way too heavy in the stomach!

Felipe: And just like that he's become unpopular ... (laughs). As to myself, I love milk chocolate, but I have to be careful, as I am only eighteen—my body is in a phase where it is getting into shape.

WHAT WAS YOUR BIGGEST FAUX PAS REGARDING NUTRITION BEFORE OR DURING A COMPETITION?

Felipe: Once I went to a fitness studio after drinking milk. Not a good combination: my body literally rebelled and I had to hurry to get back home.

Daniel: I can't afford such mistakes.

Felipe: Now he's perfect, too. This is getting out of hand (laughs).

WHAT DOES YOUR EVENING AND MORNING BEFORE A RACE LOOK LIKE? WHAT'S ON YOUR PLATE AND IN YOUR GLASS?

Daniel: I eat fruit and drink a lot of water. Because it gets so hot in the cockpit, water is extremely important.

Felipe: I keep a strict diet during the week. But before an important race I am not that tough with myself. This doesn't mean that I just wolf down whatever's in front of me.

HOW DO YOU CELEBRATE A SUCCESSFUL RACE?

Daniel: Felipe and I are quite similar: we celebrate with family and our best friends. I think the connection with family is in our Brazilian genes. Now and then we let it rip after a race. Felipe is slowly getting to the age where he's allowed to do that (laughs).

A SPECIAL RESTAURANT OR A PLACE WHERE YOU WOULD LIKE TO TAKE YOUR WIVES OR GIRLFRIENDS?

Felipe: I really like Salzburg a lot. It's so quiet here, very different than Brazil. My girlfriend should really get to know this.

Daniel: At home my wife, and I prefer to go to the restaurants that are in the immediate vicinity. Perhaps they aren't the best in the world, but I feel at home when I'm there.

WHAT CHARACTERISTIC UNITES A SUCCESSFUL PILOT AND A GOOD COOK?

Felipe: The one thing we have in common is that it looks so easy from a distance, but both racing sports and cooking require incredible discipline if you want to get to the top.

Daniel: Cooks and race car drivers have to be a bit crazy; that's not a disadvantage.

COOKING IS ...

Daniel: ... art.

Felipe: Correct. The art of making two Brazilians happy (laughs).

THE LONG WAY TO THE TOP

WITH TOMATOES, IT'S THE INSIDE THAT COUNTS.

"Don't be fooled by tomatoes," says Roland Trettl. What he means is: tomatoes can be nice and red and still taste dull. And this naturally means that the entire dish is ruined. There's only one solution: "At the store, look left and right, and when nobody's watching, take a bite!"

SPAGHETTI AL POMODORO

30 MINUTES

SCALE 3

INGREDIENTS SPAGHETTI:
160 g (5½ oz) flour
160 g (5½ oz) farina (semolina)
260 g (9 oz) egg yolk
olive oil, salt

SAUCE:
400 g (14 oz) cocktail tomatoes
ice cubes
2 onions
1/2 garlic clove
1 small chili pod
olive oil
salt
8 g (½ TBSP) sugar
tarragon
basil
thyme
20 g (¾ oz) Parmesan
pepper

The tomatoes shine red like starting lights. In a few seconds Daniel Serra and Felipe Fraga start off in the Ikarus Grand Prix. The purpose is—as always—to hold the bowl in your hands: the bowl full of delicious, homemade spaghetti.

GENTLEMEN, START YOUR ENGINES!

The tomatoes must be skinned and quartered. To facilitate things they are first placed in a pot with boiling water, then they are removed a few seconds later with a sieve and refreshed with ice cubes. But this has only a marginal effect on the speed of the two racers. "You are way too slow," teases Daniel in the general direction of Felipe, who replies coolly: "Perhaps while skinning. But you drive way too slowly."

Roland Trettl is getting ready to overtake them. Practice is what makes an executive chef. While the two continue to putter around with the tomatoes he chops the onions. A clever strategy, as those who are behind are now struggling with low visibility. The combination of salty tears and splashy tomato juice makes for fogged visors.

But a real racer isn't easily deterred; he counterattacks with garlic. Chopping it really small keeps even the toughest competitor at a distance. The same is true for the chili: its tip is cut off and it is finely chopped.

HOT PHASE

For the sauce Roland puts olive oil in a pot. Once the oil is hot the chopped onions, garlic, and chili pieces are added. When the onions are glassy the quartered tomatoes are added as well.

The resulting sauce is seasoned with salt and a little bit of sugar. "Why the sugar?," Daniel and Felipe ask, dumbfounded. "Tomatoes are always somewhat acidic. The sugar equalizes the taste," explains the master chef. Roland adds the final touch with dried tarragon, basil, and thyme leaves.

While the sauce is simmering over low heat, the three get to work on the dough for the noodles. The ingredients are mixed by hand and kneaded for about ten minutes. Roland

then puts the smooth dough through the pasta machine for as long as it takes until the dough is thin enough to be made into noodles. A tip from the chef: "The dough is perfect when it's about 3 mm (1/10") thick!"

To prepare the noodles Roland cuts the dough into four equal rectangles. Daniel and Felipe are tasked with alternating running them through the pasta machine.

Meanwhile, a large pot with boiling saltwater is waiting for the freshly-made noodles. Just as on the race track, things in the kitchen have to happen quickly now, as the fresh spaghetti requires only three minutes until it is done.

While the pasta is boiling the sauce is poured from the pot into the pan and continues to simmer at low heat. Now, grate the Parmesan and on towards the home stretch.

HOME STRETCH

Now the noodles are added to the sauce in the pan. Felipe adds some pepper while Rolands chops a few basil leaves and adds them to the mix. The pan is tossed so everything is mixed thoroughly. The Parmesan is added and the pan is tossed once again.

But this time Daniel takes command, proving he has at least as much feel for the pan as he has on the race track, because even Felipe nods with appreciation: "Nice, nice ..."

AWARD CEREMONY

Kudos from a colleague: the knightly accolade for a racer! This should settle the matter of who won, but Daniel—always the professional—clarifies: "This was teamwork of the finest kind. And after all, with Roland we have a team manager who has contributed to the success."

The pasta is placed on the plates. Roland decorates with some Parmesan and basil leaves, then follows the ceremony of eating. "This pasta is world-class!," agree both Daniel and Felipe. And it doesn't really matter that there's "only" water and not champagne being served.

SURFER

SOUTH AFRICA
RESIDENCE: CAPE TOWN

JORDY SMITH

APPETITE FOR OCEAN.

NAME: Jordan Michael Smith

NICKNAME: Jordy, J-Dog

BIRTHDAY: February 11, 1988

HEIGHT: 1.88 m (6' 1½")

WEIGHT: 93 kg (205 lbs)

DISCIPLINE: surfing competition

HOBBY: soccer

WEBSITE: www.jordysmith.com

TWITTER: @jordysmith88

What is your image of a professional surfer? Long hair bleached by the sun and saltwater? Fit, lean, and tanned? Always cool-talking? There you go, now you know Jordy Smith! Meanwhile, the South African is mentioned with surf legends such as Kelly Slater, not just because of his looks, but mostly because of his performance on the board.

But let's start at the beginning: Smith was born in Durban, and as early as 2006, he caused a furor. At eighteen he conquered the waves of the World Champion Tour daring and reckless, leaving several surfing figures in the dust, so to speak. In 2010, he was at the top of the list and won second place that same year. Major victories followed: Billabong Pro J-Bay, but he didn't land the big one—the World Championship. Experts and his competitors on the waves agree on this one issue: it's not a question whether Jordy will hold the trophy in his hands, only a matter of when.

Many experts believe Jordy Smith could start a new era with his style, something that only a few surfers have managed to do. It hasn't changed anything with respect to his unconcerned manner.

2007

1. place ASP World Qualifying Series

2010

2. place ASP World Tour;
1. place Billabong Pro, J-Bay;
2. place Quiksilver Pro, Gold Coast;
2. place Rip Curl Pro, Portugal

2011

7. place ASP World Tour;
1. place Billabong Pro, J-Bay;
3. place Quiksilver Pro, Gold Coast;
3. place Rip Curl Pro, Bells Beach;
3. place Quiksilver Pro, France

2012

5. place PRIM Mr. Price Pro, Ballito;
5. place Rip Curl Pro, Victoria;
5. place Quiksilver Pro, Gold Coast

2013

X-Games-Gold, Real Surf;
1. place Billabong Pro, Rio;
3. place Rip Curl Pro, Bells Beach

More than just a surfer: *Bending Colours* from 2012 is the second surfer movie featuring Jordy Smith.

"I'M AFRICAN. I EAT UNTIL THERE'S NOTHING LEFT."

[INTERVIEW]

WHAT MAKES YOUR DISCIPLINED ATHLETE'S HEART BECOME WEAK? WHAT DO YOU NEVER PICK UP WITH YOUR FORK?

Shellfish don't have a chance in my case, as I unfortunately have an allergy. Other than that, I'm the biggest sweet tooth under the sun; the sweet things don't get old around me.

WHAT WAS YOUR BIGGEST MISTAKE REGARDING NUTRITION BEFORE OR DURING A COMPETITION?

Right before a surfing competition in Asia I once ordered a chicken-fish-plate at a restaurant. The dish was served on a wooden plate that was probably not too clean. I donated the first half of the meal to the fish while paddling out to the waves. But the contest was over for me; I got the typical Bali belly. I even needed infusions to get back on my feet.

WHAT IS THE EVENING AND THE MORNING BEFORE A COMPETITION LIKE IN YOUR CASE? WHAT'S ON YOUR PLATE AND IN YOUR GLASS?

It's wholesome! The evening before there's always fish and salad. The morning of the competition I get up early and have a cup of coffee and a smoothie. When the competition comes close I only eat bananas and nuts.

HOW DO YOU CELEBRATE A SUCCESSFUL COMPETITION?

Pizza, Vodka Red Bull, and sex with my girlfriend.

LET'S ASSUME YOU GET A DATE FOR DINNER WITH LINDSEY VONN. WHERE WOULD YOU TAKE HER?

First I'd ask my girlfriend ... (grins, as she is sitting next to him).

YOU HAVE ONE LAST MEAL. WHAT WOULD YOU ORDER?

Chocolate pizza! Wait ... Really, the last meal? Let's see ... it would definitely have to be one of the world's best pizzas!

A LOOK INTO THE CRYSTAL BALL: WHAT COMES AFTER YOUR CAREER - MORE SIXPACK ABS OR SIX PACK ABS WITH BACON WRAP?

Oh, I'd have to be even more careful than I am now. But I can't imagine getting out of shape. I was fat once. If you know the feeling, particularly if you also know what it feels like to be slim and lightweight, you won't ever allow yourself to lose control again. At least I won't.

THE LONG WAY TO THE TOP

NEVER CUT YOUR FINGERS AGAIN.

Injuries caused by cuts are a thing of the past if you follow a basic rule: always bend the fingertips inward while cutting; the back of the fingers guide and hold the knife in place at the upper flank of the blade.

BUNNY CHOW

60 MINUTES

SCALE 4

INGREDIENTS:
300 g (10½ oz) sirloin steak
150 g (51/3 oz) red potatoes
1 onion
1 chili pod
2 garlic cloves
1 pinch of caraway
5 cardamom seeds
10 white peppercorns
5 curry leaves
oil, olive oil
2 pinches of chili powder
(Piment d'Espelette)
120 g (½ cup) lentils (precooked)
2 large tomatoes, finely chopped
salt
100 g (3½ oz) corn (can)
2 cilantro leaves
4 baguette buns

Roland Trettl's face showed how perplexed he was. He had just received the recipe for Bunny Chow from Jordy Smith's adoptive home in California. He could perfectly imagine how it would taste. But the dish itself didn't say much to the well-traveled chef.

Jordy Smith cleared up the matter when he arrived at the kitchen of Ikarus. Bunny Chow was introduced by Indian immigrants to South Africa in the area around Durban who had looked for ways of bringing curries to their mates on the plantations. This resulted in the idea of carving out baguette bread and filling it. Later on, Bunny Chow became a popular meal among workers.

Today they can be found in many snack restaurants in Smith's home town, Durban. The filling of Bunny Chow varies a lot. Vegetarian, or with pork, beef, lamb, chicken, or even surf and turf: according to Jordy, the fillings are almost without limits!

It's getting spicy!

Roland chooses beef and chops it into small cubes. Same with the red potatoes. Meanwhile, Jordy has a tearful experience while complying with Trettl tasking him to finely chop onion, chili, and garlic.

Now the master chef takes care of the spices. He crushes caraway, cardamom, white pepper, the finely chopped garlic, and the curry leaves in a mortar. Trettl adds a dash of oil so the spices bind together and are easier to chop.

In parallel, the surfer takes care of his onion and fries it in a pan with hot olive oil. Trettl's spice blend and the chili powder are added as well. Here the master chef uses the particularly intense Piment d'Espelette from the Basque Countries, causing Jordy Smith to make huge eyes. He runs to the faucet and desperately drinks water to alleviate the hotness in his mouth. "Phew! Spice Battle, I thought it's only played in Bali ..."

Once all of the ingredients are lightly braised the precooked lentils and the finely chopped tomatoes are added. Trettl adds salt and fills the pan with water until the ingredients are floating a bit. Allow this to simmer over medium heat for ten minutes.

"What is the most important ingredient when preparing meat? The meat!"

Meanwhile, it's the meat's turn. Trettl seasons the meat cubes with chili powder and salt. He then vigorously braises the beef and adds the potatoes to the pan until they are soft.

Meat and potatoes are put with the corn into the other pan to form the Chow mix. He chops cilantro leaves and mixes them with all of the ingredients. Allow the Bunny Chow to soak for one hour over low heat (not boiling!). The baguette buns are hollowed out and the Chow is filled into them.

Africa in Salzburg.

"Wow, that puts Bunny Chow on the next level," Jordy Smith sums up the cooking session after finishing the entire pot that would have satisfied four. Trettl is happy as well, about the new recipe. And one less missing piece in his cooking repertoire.

"Don't call me talented so much or I'll be the one who has to cook at home from now on."

For Jordy, Bunny Chow is "fun food." Why? Because you can eat it with your fingers and nobody complains when stuff gets spilled.

EXTREME BIKER

AUSTRIA
RESIDENCE: OBERNDORF

MARKUS STÖCKL

HERCULES IN A DOUBLE DECKER.

NAME: Markus Stöckl

NICKNAME: Hercules

BIRTHDAY: July 9, 1974

HEIGHT: 1.90 m (6' 2")

WEIGHT: 98.5 kg (217 lbs)

DISCIPLINE: speedbike

HOBBIES: my life is a hobby, cooking, biking, driving

WEBSITE: www.ms-racing.at

FACEBOOK: www.facebook.com/MSMondrakerTeam

Whether earth, snow, or gravel: whatever terrain Markus Stöckl is working with his mountain bikes, there's definitely no grass growing later on.

Whenever the robust speedbiker nicknamed "Hercules" is not reaching for a new world speed record, he is at least hunting for it. With his double decker bus and his own small team he travels around the world, searching for tracks for his last big goal: the first to crack 250 km/h (155 mph) on a production mountain bike.

The most dangerous situation in Markus Stöckl's action-packed biography has nothing to do with his profession: during a canyoning outing with a friend he fought against the raging waters for three hours—and he fought for his survival. "In this situation we saved each other's life about 100 times," says the Tyrolean in retrospect. And when you survived? "We went to have a really good dinner."

Team player: Markus Stöckl is the founder of the mountain bike team MS Racing. Together with his buddies he turned it into one of the most important and successful teams of the scene in just a few years.

1999

World speed record for production bikes: 187.013 km/h (116.204 mph) on snow, Les Arcs, French Alps

2007

World speed record for production bikes: 210.4 km/h (130.7 mph) on snow track, Chilean Andes

2011

World speed record for production mountain bikes: 164.95 km/h (102.49 mph) on sand and gravel, volcano cone of the Cerro Negro, Nicaragua.

"I AM NEVER AFRAID, REALLY."

FROZEN PIZZA CUTS NO ICE WITH HIM.

[INTERVIEW]

COOKING IS …

… like a mix of meditation and high performance sports; it requires both the mind and the body.

TRY TO COMPARE YOUR SPORT WITH A DISH. WHICH ONE COMES TO MIND?

Pork roast with crust: hard, honest, and now and then you lose a tooth. But the enjoyment is primary.

WHAT MAKES YOUR DISCIPLINED ATHLETE'S HEART BECOME WEAK? WHAT DO YOU NEVER PICK UP WITH A FORK?

There isn't really anything I don't like. But I watch out for quality; I would never eat cheap meat. I simply can't understand how someone can buy a ready-made pizza for ninety cents. I know beforehand how they dealt with the ingredients.

HOW DO YOU CELEBRATE A NEW WORLD RECORD?

With Vodka Bull. Always. But for my world record intent in Chile we almost didn't get it. Fortunately, a friend of mine found a place and reserved the last four cans. When I pocketed the world record we celebrated with it.

WHAT WAS IT YOU COULDN'T STAND AT ALL? AND DO YOU LIKE IT TODAY?

Mustard and creamy spinach. Spinach is still out of the question today, and for mustard there's got to be some sausage with it.

A RESTAURANT OR A SPECIAL PLACE WHERE YOU WANT TO HAVE DINNER?

I'm a big fan of Italian food because it is so simple and uncomplicated and yet it tastes great. So I could imagine sitting with some fresh Sicilian pasta at the crater of Mount Etna and then racing straight down into the valley!

YOU HAVE ONE LAST MEAL. WHAT WOULD YOU ORDER?

A smoked Angus beef rib. About six kilos (13 lbs) of meat should be sufficient to stave off the end for a while.

AT THE TABLE WITH FAMILY AND FRIENDS: ARE YOU THE FIRST ONE TO FINISH OR DO YOU ENJOY EVERY BITE?

I'm usually the last one to sit down as I have to do the cooking (laughs)!

A HISTORIC PERSON YOU WOULD LIKE TO TAKE OUT FOR DINNER?

I'd love to have a nice quiet dinner with my girlfriend. It's been quite a while.

THE LONG WAY TO THE TOP

RULE OF THUMB FOR FRUIT: TRY FIRST, THEN COOK.

When you cook or boil apples or other fruit you shoudn't forget to sample it while raw. Under-ripe or over-ripe fruit should not make it into the pot or the pan—the taste will definitely not improve. This might be pretty obvious, but this is a mistake even many pros commit, according to Trettl. "The apple then tastes like a napkin and you wonder …"

CARAMELIZED PAN-FRIED APPLES

30 MINUTES

SCALE 5

INGREDIENTS:

4 eggs
salt, sugar
3 apples
40 g (1½ oz) butter
15 g (1 TBSP) brown sugar
rum
100 g (3½ oz) sour cream
250 g (8¾ oz) curd
25 g (¾ oz) farina (semolina)
1 orange zest
1 lemon zest
80 g (1/3 cup) grated hazelnuts
5 g (1 tsp) starch
60 g (¼ cup) icing sugar
30 g (1 oz) milk
10 g (1/3 oz) flour
30 g (1 oz) pine or pistachio nuts
1 pinch of cinnamon

We've met before somewhere ... nice when you discover that you have something in common in your past. Even if it is limited to a few hours: in the case of Markus Stöckl and Roland Trettl, it was an overseas flight when they sat next to each other and started chatting.

"Back then you were terribly agitated about the in-flight food," remembers Markus, and Roland replies with a smirk: "I am not surprised at all."

Even today the two can talk about cooking, as the speedbiker is quite experienced in this matter. As a trained cook he brings with him the necessary foundation to not be completely at the mercy of the Ikarus chef.

The other thing he's bringing along is the recipe for pan-fried apples, which was his favorite meal at his grandma's when he was just a kid. "A real challenge for me," remarks Trettl, "as I usually don't prepare sweet dishes; that's a job for the patisserie." Markus has to laugh: "A clear case of understatement. I'm sure you will manage somehow."

First step: the egg white has to be whipped. This is usually done with a blender, but Roland and Markus want to take matters into their own hands, literally.

"See who is faster!"

Roland has caught the fever of competition: power meets technique. In one corner, the powerhouse from Tirol with a forearm circumference of some fifty centimeters (19.5"). In the other corner, the precision mechanic from South Tirol: steet-wise, focused, and with a wealth of experience from the world's best kitchens. GONG!

They both stir their bowl making strenuous faces. And it looks like power is taking the lead. After barely a minute Markus raises his hands. Done! Or not quite? On close inspection it turns out the egg white is more like concrete. The muscleman has definitely gone too far ...

"What are you? Man or machine?!" ...

... Roland can't believe it. And while he calmly whips his egg white he has a tip: "Add a pinch of salt to the egg white; it provides the right stability, and just before getting the right consistency, add some sugar for the flavor."

After a short break Markus and Roland start peeling the apples. One of them is cut into small cubes, the other two into finger-thick slices. Roland then heats some butter in an uncoated deep pan and adds the apple pieces. He lightly braises them for a few minutes with some brown sugar sprinkled over them and then deglazes them with a dash of rum.

The dough is prepared by mixing the flour with sour cream, curd, semolina, and cinnamon in a bowl, adding sugar, and mixing in the egg yolk. To add taste, Markus grates orange and lemon zests over it. Now the grated hazelnuts are added as well and the dough is thickened with some starch. Then the egg white is folded in.

A different deep and uncoated pan is heated with butter in it and the apple slices are sugared and briefly braised. "Are they brown already?," Markus asks impatiently. "Now we can finally add the dough!" He spreads out the dough evenly over the apple slices inside the pan. Roland adds the fried apple pieces over it.

Suddenly the supposedly inexperienced sweet dish cook remembers something: "You know what would fit this dish perfectly?," asks Roland, not waiting for an answer. "Pine nuts!"

Overturned: Markus' egg white can be turned upside down, but not eaten.

But Trettl has a minor inconvenience regarding his own restaurant. Despite the fact that the Ikarus patisserie section features an entire wall of ingredients, the container of pine nuts is empty.

"Doesn't matter, pistachios work just as well"—the master chef has already made his plan B. With the green nuts as the topping the pan is placed into the oven preheated to 165 degrees (325°F) and stays there for about twenty minutes, or for as long as it takes the dough to take on a nice brown color.

Now some 10 g (1/3 oz) of icing sugar is sprinkled over it, where it caramelizes because of the heat of the dough—then the "Apfelschmarren" (pan-fried apples) is done.

The kitchen chef doesn't recommend the usual coffee or glass of milk to go with the sweet dish. "If you like, just go ahead," says Roland Trettl. "But a better choice would be something fresh and mildly fruity."

At home outdoors: Roland and Markus enjoy the meal at the outdoor lounge of Hangar-7.

TEAM SPIRIT WITH TAURINE.

Into a new era! This applied to both Red Bull and the EC Salzburg at the turn of the millennium. Taking over the ice hockey club in 2000 was the first engagement with a team sport by Red Bull. Success came soon—just as did more team sport projects that Red Bull has pursued with much ambition and vision. By now there are soccer clubs in New York, Salzburg, Leipzig, and Brazil running the flag of Red Bull. In 2012, the German ice hockey league received a club with new wings: EHC Red Bull München is now challenging the well-established teams of Berlin, Düsseldorf, and Cologne.

MATTHIAS TRATTNIG / ALEXANDER BARTA

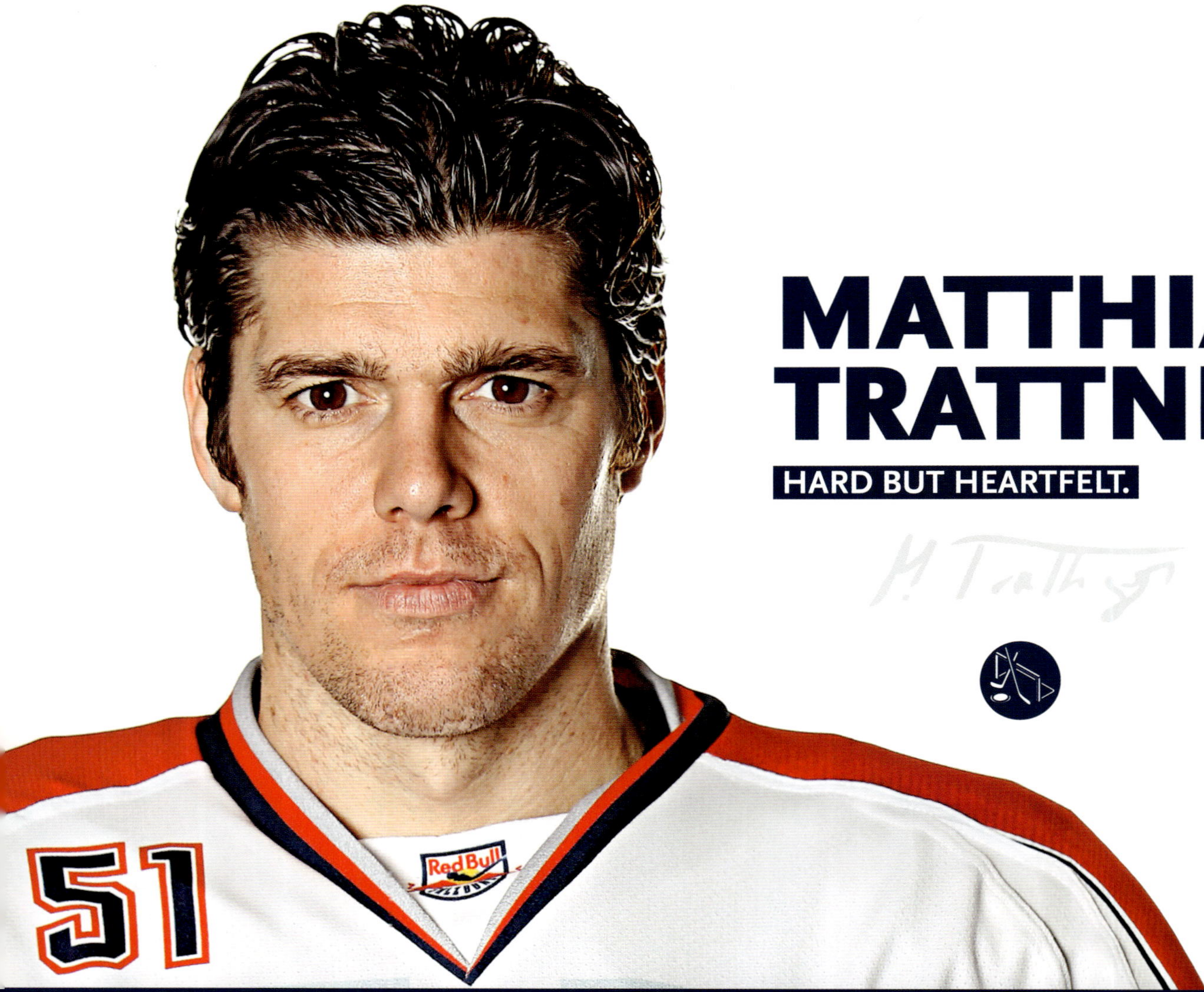

MATTHIAS TRATTNIG

HARD BUT HEARTFELT.

NAME: Matthias Trattnig

NICKNAME: Tratte

BIRTHDAY: April 22, 1979

HEIGHT: 1.85 m (6')

WEIGHT: 96 kg (211 lbs)

HOBBIES: kitesurfing, tennis, golf

WEBSITE: www.redbulls.com

His enemies label him "unpredictable." His colleagues say "positively crazy." And the cold statistics say that this uncompromising defensive player was never short of penalty minutes. But the same goes for victories. In over fifteen years of professional ice hockey, a couple of things have kept piling up: four Austrian Championships with EC Red Bull Salzburg, where he has been an indispensable team member since 2005. Before that his path led him away from his home town Graz into the US College League and later into the American Hockey League (AHL), on to Sweden to Djurgardens IF, and into the German Ice Hockey League (DEL) to Kassel. But Matthias Trattnig never felt as comfortable as when he was in Salzburg. Because, in private, number 51 is a down-to-earth family man. The unforgiving version is only available on the ice.

Inhibited restaurateur: Matthias Trattnig's parents run a hotel right next to Lake Wörth. "But that's not really my thing, and I never worked there. They wouldn't have had much use for me anyway."

2002
Olympia participation (Austria)

2007
Austrian Champion (EC Red Bull Salzburg)

2008
Austrian Champion (EC Red Bull Salzburg)

2010
Austrian Champion (EC Red Bull Salzburg)

2011
European Trophy winner (EC Red Bull Salzburg)

ICE HOCKEY PLAYER

AUSTRIA
RESIDENCE: SALZBURG

ALEXANDER BARTA

BERLIN BIGMOUTH SHARPSHOOTER.

NAME: Alexander Barta

NICKNAME: Barts

BIRTHDAY: February 2, 1983

HEIGHT: 1.79 m (5' 9")

WEIGHT: 80 kg (176 lbs)

HOBBIES: fashion and tennis

WEBSITE: www.redbullmuenchen.de

A center player in ice hockey has one particular task: he has to be cold as ice in front of the goal. So Alexander Barta is perfect for this position. This player born in Berlin not only satisfies his fans with his cool talk, but also with goals, ever since he stepped into the DEL in 2001. In 2005, he won the German championship with the Eisbären (polar bears) Berlin, and he was the captain of the Hamburg Freezers for five years. As part of the German National Team he caused a stir in the opposite goal area over a hundred times. He promises that this will not change after two years in Sweden and the switch to EHC Red Bull Munich: "Munich and Red Bull are up to something big. I'll do my part."

Duel of brothers: Björn—older brother of Alex Barta—also plays ice hockey in the DEL and plays for the Bavarian rival of Red Bull Munich, Ingolstadt. "This duel will be something really special for us."

2005

German Champion (Eisbären Berlin), World Championship participation (Germany)

2006

Olympic participation (Germany)

ICE HOCKEY PLAYER

GERMANY
RESIDENCE: MUNICH

Big expectations: "Alex is without a doubt the best German center-forward," says the manager of EHC Red Bull Munich, Christian Winkler, about the new addition.

Loudspeaker: Matthias Trattnig doesn't hold back his opinions, even if he gets into trouble. "That's the way I am, and as the captain, it's my job."

HAVING A DRINK WITH MARIO BASLER.

[INTERVIEW]

WHAT IS THE EVENING AND THE MORNING BEFORE A GAME LIKE WITH YOU GUYS? WHAT'S ON YOUR PLATES AND IN YOUR GLASSES?

Alex: granola and yogurt for breakfast. Then there's the final training. For lunch, we hit our favorite Italian restaurant where we get salad and noodles. Right before the game the only thing I might drink is coffee, because I imagine that I play better.

Matthias: I always drink coffee, too, but for a different reason. I have to go to the bathroom and loosen up (laughs).

WHAT WAS IT YOU COULDN'T STAND AS KIDS? AND DO YOU LIKE IT TODAY?

Alex: I never liked olives when I was younger, but now I like them a lot But I can't get used to tomatoes, not yet.

Matthias: I don't like tomatoes, either. And snails—but I'm definitely not the only one.

AT THE TABLE WITH FAMILY AND FRIENDS: ARE YOU THE FIRST ONES TO FINISH THEIR PLATE OR DO YOU ENJOY EVERY BITE?

Matthias: I'm one of those who is done in seconds while the other guys are still working on their soup.

Alex: I'm not really known as a connoisseur, either ...

BEER IN THE GARDEN OR A GLASS OF WINE AT THE BAR?

Matthias: Why the "or?"

Alex: Both. However, if I really had to choose between the two I would pick a nice glass of white wine.

HOW DO YOU CELEBRATE A SUCCESSFUL GAME?

Matthias: As an ice hockey player you have quite a few successful games during the season if you aren't playing on the wrong team, so you might be sitting with team colleagues having a beer. But when you can celebrate a championship ... well, hello! That's when things get really interesting.

Alex: I personally look forward to the Oktoberfest in Munich. We'll definitely go there when we have something to celebrate.

Matthias: Last year we had planned this as well—it's not too far from Salzburg after all. And then we lost the game before that. Man, the trainer was really furious! And the outing was canceled.

A FAMOUS SPORTSMAN YOU WOULD LIKE TO HAVE DINNER WITH?

Matthias: The standard reply from an ice hockey player: Wayne Gretzky. To sit at the same table with this legend is a dream for any professional my age. Are you old enough to know him, Alex? (laughs)

Alex: I am young enough to play cat and mouse with him! But seriously: I'd love to have dinner with Mario Basler. For one, because of him I became a fan of Bayern. And second, because it would be fun to go out for a drink after dinner. (laughs)

THE LONG WAY TO THE TOP

COOKING RICE WITH A SPECIAL TOUCH.

Even the most passionate top chefs rely on technology at times if it serves a purpose. "Rice will rarely turn out as well in the pot as it does with a rice cooker," says Roland Trettl. Although even in this case a good feel and touch is helpful—in the very sense of the word. "In the rice cooker, the water should always be about a fingertip above the rice. This will make it perfect, guaranteed."

SUSHI

60 MINUTES

SCALE 10

INGREDIENTS:
(AMOUNT VARIES DEPENDING ON YOUR TASTE!)

- 300 g (1¼ cups) sushi rice
- 2 TBSP rice vinegar
- 1 tsp mirin (Japanese rice wine)
- 4 soft shell crabs
- tempura dough (from Asian food stores)
- oil for deep frying
- 150 g (5 1/3 oz) salmon
- 150 g (5 1/3 oz) tuna
- 100 g (3½ oz) shrimp
- 1 mango
- 1 cucumber
- 2 avocados
- 8 nori leaves
- soy sauce
- wasabi paste
- 1 bunch of chives

SUSHI BOX

The origin of sushi is not Japan, but Southeast Asia. This is where freshwater fish from the Mekong were pickled with rice to conserve it. The rice was later discarded, until it was realized that the rice, which had become sour due to fermentation, actually tasted quite good with the fish.

The modern variant of sushi was developed during the nineteenth century in Tokyo, where saltwater fish were used as filling for the first time. It took until 1950 for a Japanese immigrant to open the first sushi restaurant in the West, in Los Angeles.

THE TWO MOST WELL-KNOWN TYPES OF SUSHI

NIGIRI

means "ball" for a good reason: when preparing Nigiri sushi, rice is shaped into a small, longish ball and covered with fish or seafood. Sometimes a strip of nori (algae leaf) is used to affix the fish.

MAKI

means "roll," and here as well the name says it all. Maki sushi are rolls of rice wrapped in a leaf of nori that are filled at their center with raw fish, seafood, and vegetables. Rolling is best done with a bamboo mat. There are several subsets of Maki sushi.

HERE ARE THE MOST IMPORTANT ONES:

HOSO-MAKI: thin and made from half a nori leaf, filled with only one ingredient: fish or vegetables.

FUTO-MAKI: thick and made from an entire nori leaf, filled with various ingredients, depending on the cook's preference.

URA-MAKI: also known in the West as a "California Roll." Ura maki is rolled "the wrong way," so there is no nori leaf on the outside, just rice. It is often decorated with sesame seed or colored fish eggs.

THE THREE BIG SUSHI SINS

1. EATING SUSHI WITH CHOPSTICKS

In Japan, sushi is traditionally eaten with your fingers and as whole pieces. Biting off a piece of sushi is a no-no.

2. MIXING SOY SAUCE AND WASABI

A Japanese would never do this. Soy sauce and wasabi are served separately on the plate.

3. DIPPING SUSHI INTO THE SOY SAUCE WITH THE RICE SIDE FIRST

If at all, in Japan only the fish side is used, or you might simply drip some soy sauce onto the sushi.

"Referee" Roland Trettl calls the shots; there is no clemency with respect to the two ice hockey cracks.

The last time Matthias Trattnig and Alex Barta faced each other it ended with an earthquake. A sports earthquake, but nevertheless ...

In February 2013, Trattnig got the ticket for the Olympic Games with the Austrian ice hockey team: during a nerve-racking, defining game against the big favorite Germany, featuring Alex Barta.

New fuel for an old rivalry thirty-five years after Córdoba. Córdoba? Ask any Austrian, he will tell you all about it.

"... to this day I don't know how it could happen," says Barta, who still feels the sting. "Usually we should have won the game, but that day we just couldn't score." "Simply because you couldn't get past our defense," explains Trattnig, who can't suppress a defiant grin.

It is good that Roland Trettl, being Italian, is neutral here and intervenes as a referee. In his youth, the executive chef of Ikarus was a passionate ice hockey player. The fact that his strength was mostly on the penalty bench is not brought up when he asks his two guests for a handshake at the stove.

"Be nice and wash your hands," the cook imitates a strict referee. Not without a second thought, as Trettl is visualizing the preparation of shushi, for which clean hands are indispensable.

The sushi rice is also washed well before it is put into the rice cooker. Trettl: "This special rice has a lot of starch, of which a portion must be removed. Otherwise it would be way too sticky."

Once the rice is done it is placed in a large bowl and fanned until it has cooled down—because of the look of it. "The faster the rice cools down the more shiny it is later on. So, gentlemen, get fanning and presto!"

He doesn't have to say this twice to the two ice hockey cracks; they have plenty of power in their arms anyway. After a few minutes the rice is ready to be mixed with rice vinegar and mirin, which provides necessary acidity.

Why did the two pick sushi? "It's hot enough already on the ice, so I'd rather have something cold with Matthias," laughs Alex. This is perfectly fine with Trattnig, as he has become a "great fan of sushi" since he spent time in the US. The choice of restaurants is much larger than in Salzburg, "but even here I often go to eat sushi with team members. We have our special places."

He moves on to put the softshell crabs (with the shell) into flour and then rolls them on a plate in the tempura dough. "These are going to be spider rolls, my favorite sushi," Matthias explains the special term for the maki rolls to his wide-eyed colleague, which are filled with baked crabs.

This is the keyword for the next step of the recipe,where the crab is put into the deep fryer. A last timeout before the all-important final third begins.

Powerplay on the bamboo mat.

Alex and Matthias carefully cut the fish and the vegetables into maki-compliant long and thin strips. Now the great sushi rolling can commence.

Roland has prepared the small bamboo mat on the countertop and covered it with cling wrap. Now the three of them place one nori leaf on it with about one handful of rice at the center.

"Real sushi masters even count the number of rice grains they use for each piece," Roland recounts. "But we can do with our sense of proportion: just take a handful!"

The way the ingredients are combined with rice is entirely up to the cooks. Matthias chooses mango and tuna for his first roll. Alex goes for shrimp and avocado, while Roland grabs the salmon.

Nobody has to be afraid of rolling, says Trettl: "Many believe they can't do it, but it's totally irrelevant how you roll. The important thing is that the rice and nori leaves are of good quality."

Another tip from the chef: "If you want to make sure you got it right just check it out on YouTube: there are plenty of videos showing how perfect rolling is done."

With increasing practice Matthias and Alex are getting faster. More and more maki rolls are piling up on the wooden board, where they are later cut into bite-sized pieces and served with soy sauce and wasabi.

Even before the sound of the final buzzer is heard the referee lays out his analysis: "In the case of Matthias you can tell that he's done it a few times already. In Alex's case things were a bit bumpy at first, but then while making the maki rolls you showed some really good executive qualities."

With so many compliments and the perfect sushi, the loss against Austria is easier to stomach ...

Alex on the attack: "Roland, somehow cooks always look better on TV."

COOK

ITALY
RESIDENCE: BAD REICHENHALL, GERMANY

ROLAND TRETTL

TAKING HITS. DEALING BLOWS. AND COOKING DAMN WELL.

NAME: Roland Trettl

BIRTHDAY: July 3, 1971

HEIGHT: 1.83 m (6')

WEIGHT: 93 kg (205 lbs)

HOBBY: fashion

WEBSITE: www.hangar-7.com

Whether Australia, Mexico, or Hong Kong and Thailand, the life of Roland Trettl is a constant arrival and departure. The unique concept of Ikarus keeps its executive chef busy: each month he visits future guest cooks in their home city or country. But Trettl nevertheless has a firm grip on "his" restaurant.

His recipe for success: he thinks like a top athlete, constantly looking for total perfection. The born South Tyrolian takes advantage of his past as an ice hockey crack. He can take hits, he can deal blows—and he is also a committed team player. These are qualities that the elite cook Eckart Witzigmann appreciated when he suggested him for Ikarus in 2003. "The best job in the world," says Roland Trettl about his job in Salzburg. Close to the restaurant, he also relaxes privately after his long trips—if his young son allows him to.

1992
Aubergine, Munich

1994
Tantris Restaurant, Munich

1997
Ca's Puers, Mallorca

2002
Marine Terrace, Tokyo

SINCE 2003
Ikarus Restaurant, Hangar-7, Salzburg

Tough but fair: as the executive chef Roland Trettl demands total perfection from his team, but meanwhile, good vibes don't take a back seat.

DINNER WITH JESUS.

[INTERVIEW]

WHICH CHARACTERISTIC UNITES A GOOD COOK WITH A SUCCESSFUL ATHLETE?

The motivation to look past the limits.

WHAT EXCITES EVEN THE JADED PALATE OF A MASTER CHEF? AND WHAT DO YOU NEVER PICK UP WITH A FORK?

I become weak with whatever is good. Anything that's bad bothers me.

WHAT WAS THE CRAZIEST THING YOU EVER ATE?

I could fill an entire evening with stories. But if you want the best ones: guinea pig in Peru, dog in Beijing, snake in Shanghai, and french fries with sauce in Brussels.

THE TASTE OF YOUR CHILDHOOD IS ...

... mashed bananas. My mom always took care of my well-being (laughs).

AT THE TABLE WITH FAMILY AND FRIENDS: ARE YOU THE FIRST ONE TO FINISH OR DO YOU ENJOY EVERY BITE?

I enjoy things express.

WHAT CAN BE FOUND IN YOUR FREEZER?

Ice cubes. Other than that I only cook with really fresh ingredients; I'm just too spoiled due to my profession.

WHICH THREE LIVING OR HISTORIC PEOPLE ARE SITTING AT THE TABLE OF YOUR PERFECT DINNER?

Leonardo da Vinci, because not only was he a grandiose artist, but also a pretty smart guy. Casanova, because every man can learn something from him. And Jesus! I would ask him at dinner what he thinks about his church.

YOU HAVE ONE LAST MEAL. WHAT WOULD YOU ORDER?

Overcooked spaghetti and beef filet "well done" with a latte macchiato. In other words, a complete culinary perversion. The worse the food the easier the departure.

YOGA À LA TRETTL

"If we are going to cook here you've got to do some sports!"

It was extreme skiing mountaineer Axel Naglich who ordered his pal Roland Trettl to exercise a bit for the *Red Bull Athlete's Cookbook*. A joke among friends turned into something more serious. Well, sort of, as these images prove.

Roland Trettl is not amused about people dismissing yoga or saying it is worthless as a sport. "If you say that you have no idea. You can't get what you get during an hour of yoga in a gym. You get really fit, but you aren't exhausted, you just feel great."

For five years Trettl has performed the exercises almost every day. Even on a plane, whenever he is traveling long distance. "I just do the exercises in the aisle."

The first improvements appear very quickly, according to the executive chef. "Not only do you get more flexibility, you are also much more relaxed. Cooks in particular have problems with posture, as they are constantly leaning forward when they are working."

His wife passed on the yoga fever to him. The professional yoga instructor taught Roland all of the postures and movements—without the knives, of course.

These are Roland's four basic rules for yoga dummies: "Chest forward. Belly inward. Shoulders backward. And smile!"

THE LONG WAY TO THE TOP SPECIAL

SOUR IS ON THE MENU!

So you did everything right while cooking, only to fail with the greens? Roland Trettl presents his four favorite dressings and their ingredients. Simply blend in a bowl and done!

VINAIGRETTE "ASIA"

INGREDIENTS:

50 g (¼ cup) brown sugar
75 g (2½ oz) lime juice
5 g (1 tsp) chopped ginger
5 g (1 tsp) chopped chili
50 g (1¾ oz) soy sauce
40 g (11/3 oz) grape seed oil

VINAIGRETTE "PUMPKIN SEED"

INGREDIENTS:

50 g (¼ cup) mustard
30 g (1 oz) creamy horseradish
10 g (2 tsp) chopped pumpkin seeds
30 g (2 TBSP) water
40 g (11/3 oz) apple vinegar
80 g (5½ TBSP) pumpkin seed oil
salt, pepper, 1 pinch of sugar

VINAIGRETTE "VINEGAR & OIL"

INGREDIENTS:

90 g (6 TBSP) old balsamic vinegar
45 g (3 TBSP) young balsamic vinegar
75 g (5 TBSP) olive oil
75 g (5 TBSP) grape seed oil
5 g salt (1 tsp), 1 pinch of sugar

VINAIGRETTE "PARMESAN"

INGREDIENTS:

2 egg yolks
50 g (1¾ oz) white wine vinegar
10 g (2 tsp) Parmesan
30 g (2 TBSP) water
80 g (5½ oz) olive oil
50 g (¼ cup) sour cream
salt and pepper

RACECAR DRIVER

NETHERLANDS
RESIDENCE: DRONTEN

BEITSKE VISSER

ON THE TRACKS OF VETTEL.

NAME: Beitske Visser

NICKNAME: Beits

BIRTHDAY: March 10, 1995

HEIGHT: 1.74 m (5' 7")

WEIGHT: 61 kg (134 lbs)

DISCIPLINE: Formula Masters

HOBBIES: carting, fitness training

WEBSITE: www.beitskevisser.com

"There's only one goal: winning!," writes Beitske Visser on her website. Actually, there is another big project in the young life of the ambitious Dutch: she wants to be the first woman to compete in Formula 1. The way to this goal is determination, motivation, and speed. After top scores in the carting division, Beitske Visser entered the first Formula class in 2012. In her first ADAC Formula Masters season she promptly celebrated two victories. Since 2013, she has driven for the Red Bull Junior Team, where Sebastian Vettel was once under contract. The perfect conditions for making history.

2010

2. place WSK Euro Series – KZ2
1. place WSK Masters Series – KZ2

2011

1. place Dutch Supercar Challenge

2012

2 victories ADAC Formula Masters

"Motor sports—this unique feeling of reaching the limit!"

ENJOY YOUR MEAL, KIMI!

[INTERVIEW]

WHAT MAKES YOUR DISCIPLINED ATHLETE'S HEART BECOME WEAK? WHAT DO YOU NEVER PICK UP WITH A FORK?

A bun with Nutella in the morning! I just can't resist it. Other than that I am pretty picky about food. I never liked fast food, for example, not even as a child.

WHAT WAS THE CRAZIEST THING YOU EVER ATE?

Some people think it's crazy that I put banana on my Nutella bun.

WHAT WAS YOUR BIGGEST FAUX PAS REGARDING NUTRITION BEFORE OR DURING A RACE?

Before each race I eat pasta with chicken. And I really mean always! So I never had such an experience.

YOU HAVE ONE LAST MEAL. WHAT WOULD YOU ORDER?

Wortelschotel, so, this is the dish I will be cooking with Roland. This is my absolute favorite dish. And for dessert, banana split.

THE TASTE OF YOUR CHILDHOOD ...

... not a big difference from today. After all, I'm still young (laughs).

WHAT CAN BE FOUND IN YOUR FREEZER?

Oops, I don't have one at home. But there's plenty of fruit, yogurt, and cheese in my fridge.

WHICH FAMOUS SPORTSMAN/ SPORTSWOMAN WOULD YOU INVITE FOR DINNER?

Kimi Räikkönen. He's such a crazy guy and as a racecar driver he is really something!

SWEET OR SOUR?

Sweet! I could do without anything except for my Nutella bun.

HOW DO YOU CELEBRATE A SUCCESSFUL RACE?

With so much ice cream that I'll get sick.

THE LONG WAY TO THE TOP

STEWING: THE SMALL DIFFERENCE.

Stewing is appropriate for long-fiber beef, as well as vegetables with an intense taste, such as carrots or tomatoes. This cooking method consists of two steps. First, a brief and vigorous braising of the ingredient in hot oil or fat. Second: cooking the closed pot over low heat. The resulting steam contributes to the cooking process. "The decisive factor is to use only a little fluid for stewing," explains Roland Trettl. "The bottom should be barely covered. Not more than that." If too much fluid is used the stewing turns into boiling—a small but an important difference that significantly changes the taste.

80 MINUTES

SCALE 5

INGREDIENTS:
600 g (21 oz) ground beef
150 g (51/3 oz) leek
200 g (7 oz) whipped cream
400 g (14 oz) carrots
10 g (2 tsp) parsley
150 g (½ cup) poultry stock
1 kg (2¼ lbs) mashed potatoes
90 g (1/3 cup) Parmesan
1 slice of butter
olive oil
salt
pepper

WORTEL-SCHOTEL

Together with her mother Jantina, Beitske Visser steps into Hangar-7. Not because the teenager would need any companionship—due to her sport and associated travel around half the world Beitske is perhaps more independent than most of her peers.

No, Jantina Visser has joined her for a different reason. She has the full confidence of her daughter regarding her favorite dish Wortelschotel, which means "bowl of carrots." Well, at least you know what you get.

"You Dutch people were never very famous for your culinary creativity" ...

... Roland Trettl laughs when Beitske and Jantina explain the dish to him. "But I think it's fabulous that we are preparing a regional dish. Could I suggest a minor detail? How about some Parmesan on top?"

Here's the Italian master chef showing his colors once again. "I never tried it, but it sounds great," Beitske agrees after a quizzical look at her mother, then starts peeling the carrots and cutting them into 1 cm (½") thick slices.

Meanwhile, Roland got himself a knife and cuts the leek. He puts it in a deep pan with hot olive oil, adds some salt, and pours the poultry stock over the fried leek. He adds a dash of whipped cream and allows it to simmer for a few minutes over low heat until the leek is soft.

The carrots that Beitske chopped are also put in a deep pan with olive oil and salt is added, and about 50 g (¼ cup) of poultry stock. "Of course you can use water as well," explains Roland, "but this is better for taste." He then puts aluminum foil over the pan and allows the carrots to stew.

While the two are waiting until the fluid inside the pan has evaporated, Beitske prepares the mashed potatoes—and wonders why Roland also uses the packs from the supermarket. "I always thought that a master chef would do it by hand with a potato masher and so on ..."

"That's what I do,' Roland replies with a wink. "But I didn't want to demand too much of you. And there's nothing to be said against the taste of mashed potatoes from the supermarket."

The carrots are done at the same time as the mashed potatoes, which Roland seasons with parsley. Then the two of them take care of the ground beef, which is fried in a pan with hot olive oil, seasoned with salt and pepper, and then mixed with the carrots. "It's not a bad idea to sample it again," Roland suggests. "After all, we don't want our tongue to fall asleep when we eat."

Now the meat with the carrots is put in the soufflé dish, then Roland spreads out the mashed potatoes and the Parmesan. Then it's the fried leek's turn, along with the rest of the poultry stock, butter, salt, and pepper to be put into the blender and the resulting mass is placed into the soufflé dish.

"Now it needs to go into the oven heated to 150 degrees (300°F) for

Roland evenly spreads out the mashed potatoes over the soufflé dish with the icing bag. You don't have one at home? No excuses, says the cook: "You can build one yourself. Simply google it."

about forty minutes. Is that about right?," Roland hollers towards Jantina Visser, who has made herself comfortable at the table, watching the action from a safe distance.

Her thumbs-up says it all:

Everything's gone according to the master chef's plan.

ALPINE SKIER

USA
RESIDENCE: VAIL

LINDSEY VONN

A CLASS OF HER OWN

NAME: Lindsey Vonn

BIRTHDAY: October 18, 1984

HEIGHT: 1.78 m (5' 8")

DISCIPLINE: downhill, Super-G, giant slalom, combination, slalom

HOBBIES: tennis, golf, road biking, reading, Law & Order TV series

WEBSITE: www.lindseyvonn.com

TWITTER: @lindseyvonn

This woman applied at the International Ski Federation (FIS) to be allowed to start at the men's race in Lake Louise. Nothing describes Lindesy Vonn's attitude better than this story. She is not afraid of exposing herself and has complete trust in her own strengths. While many wrote it off as a PR stunt, the driving force behind Lindsey's project was to reach for the next level, to explore her own limits, and to compete with the best.

Her extraordinary talent was recognized and encouraged while she was still a young child. Her three medals at the Junior World Championships stoked hopes for a successful career. She stood on the World Cup podium for the first time during the 2003/2004 season, and she turned the podium into her regular spot. Today, she is the most successful American ski racer of all time. But that's not enough for Lindsey. She wants to become the skier with the most World Cup victories. Even if the FIS turned down her request to participate in the men's race. Even if a serious knee injury prevented her from competing at the World Championship in Schladming in 2013. If you know Lindsey, you have no doubt she will get what she wants.

OLYMPIC GAMES VANCOUVER 2010

Gold – downhill
Bronze – Super-G

WORLD CHAMPIONSHIPS

2 x Gold: Val-d'Isère 2009, downhill and Super-G;
3 x Silver: Garmisch Partenkirchen 2011, downhill, Åre 2007 – downhill and Super-G

59 WORLD CUP VICTORIES
4 x OVERALL WORLD CUP WINNER
6 x DOWNHILL WORLD CUP WINNER
4 x SUPER-G WORLD CUP WINNER
3 x COMBINED WORLD CUP WINNER

Extremely low position in curves and on icy tracks. Jumps at 120 km/h (75 mph). Are you nervous? "No, not at all. When driving a car you also get used to the speed," says Lindsey. But you never get used to winning. "That's always awesome, each time."

IDEAL LINE FOR LIFE.

[INTERVIEW]

WHO ARE THE FOUR (STILL LIVING OR HISTORIC) PERSONS SITTING AT THE TABLE OF YOUR PERFECT DINNER?

Harrison Ford, because he is so incredibly cool. My boyfriend, of course. And my sisters Karin and Laura, because they are a lot of fun and we always have a good time.

WHICH FAMOUS SPORTSMAN/ SPORTSWOMAN WOULD YOU LIKE TO GO OUT TO DINNER WITH?

Roger Federer. He is one of my big idols, as a person and as a sportsman. He is the best at his sport and has been over a long time, and yet he is likable and has remained down-to-earth. He also puts a lot of effort into his charity organization, which is just unbelievable.

THE TASTE OF YOUR CHILDHOOD IS ...

... Fruity Pebbles, a cereal! Probably pure sugar, but soooo good!

WHAT DO YOU EAT BEFORE A SKI RACE?

The evening before it's salmon with rice and vegetables. Before the race itself, usually eggs.

SWEET OR SOUR?

I just say "banana bread." Sweet, of course!

WHAT WAS THE CRAZIEST THING YOU EVER ATE?

A piece from the end of a conch shell, a large ocean snail. Looks terrible, but it tastes great.

WHAT WAS IT YOU COULDN'T STAND AT ALL AS A CHILD? AND DO YOU LIKE IT TODAY?

I hated broccoli. Today I can sort of handle it when there's plenty of olive oil and garlic in it.

AT THE TABLE WITH FAMILY AND FRIENDS: ARE YOU THE FIRST ONE TO FINISH OR DO YOU ENJOY EVERY BITE?

I am always the first to finish up. Look, I am the oldest of five children! The faster you eat the better your chances for seconds.

WHICH CHARACTERISTIC UNITES A SUCCESSFUL SKI RACER WITH A GOOD COOK?

Both of them always have to see the ideal line. They have to know where they want to go.

DOESN'T IT GET BORING AT SOME POINT TO ALWAYS BE WINNING, OR AT LEAST BECOME NORMAL?

No, winning is always awesome. Besides, I don't have the most victories yet. The record stands at sixty-two, and I want to get it.

COOKING IS ...

... the question should be: Baking is ____? Then I can answer it. So: baking is relaxation. Because anything having to do with cutting is tension and stress for me!"

THE LONG WAY TO THE TOP

STRUGGLING WITH BURNT CAKE BASES.

Once cake and pie bases are burnt they are difficult to remove from the baking dish. A simple trick can prevent this. Place baking paper under an open baking dish ring. Usually two sheets of paper overlapping at the bottom are sufficient to seal the dish so the dough will not filter through. Place everything in the baking dish, add the dough, and it's off to the oven! The ring can later be lifted from the cake, simply pull off the paper.

LINZER CAKE MEETS BANANA BREAD

80 MINUTES

SCALE 4

LINZER CAKE:
75 g (1/3 cup) icing sugar
90 g (3¼ oz) butter
1 pinch of cinnamon
1 pinch of nutmeg
1/3 pulp of a vanilla pod
40 g (1½ oz) egg yolk
lemon peel
60 g (2 oz) egg white
75 g (1/3 cup) grated hazelnuts
currant jam
20 g (4 tsp) almond chips
60 g (¼ cup) sugar
75 g (1/3 cup) flour

BANANA BREAD:
4 ripe bananas
7 TBSP sugar
2 eggs
5 TBSP flour
1 pinch of cinnamon
1 pinch of nutmeg
1 tsp baking powder
1 pinch of salt
50 g (1¾ oz) chocolate chips
5 TBSP apple sauce
2 TBSP sugar

Definitely more of a confectioner than a cook. Want to try? Here are the follow-ups of Lindsey's chart: second place French toast. Root beer with frozen yogurt comes in third.

We owe the only cake in this book to Lindsey Vonn's former Austrian trainer. Due to the phonetic similarity with her name he gave her the nickname "Linzer Cake." "If that's my name I want to know how the recipe works."

Roland Trettl is nervous, something he exhibits very rarely. The reason? The answer is not more than a murmur. For one it's the guest cook Lindsey Vonn; definitely one of the most radiant sports ladies in high-performance sports today. On the other hand, it's the baking itself. Let's call it one of Trettl's lesser developed sides. With a look at the list of ingredients, the executive chef realizes the last time he dealt with "something like this" was thirty years ago, so the day before he ran a dress rehearsal with a pastry cook. Premiere for an athlete's cooking session.

The recipe for a fitting nickname.

And then occurs what happens so many times. The star arrives, but without any airs and graces. Lindsey Vonn just left her rehab training which helps her overcome the cruciate ligament rupture she suffered during the World Championship in Schladming. She brings along a good appetite, so they get baking right away.

Lindsey's first task: mixing icing sugar and butter with the hand mixer. She then adds a pinch of cinnamon, nutmeg, and vanilla pulp. Egg yolk is also added, and she grates the lemon peel over the cake dough. Meanwhile, Trettl whips the egg whites, adds sugar, and hands it to the skier, who gradually folds it into the dough, together with the hazelnuts. Vonn puts about ¾ of the dough in the baking tin and evenly spreads the jam across the top of the dough.

Trettl rolls out the rest of the dough and cuts it into narrow strips that he places onto the jam like a lattice. He adds almonds to the top and puts it into the oven preheated to 175 degrees (325°F). "And now?," says the American, looking more hungry by the minute. A baking time of forty-five minutes equals waiting time.

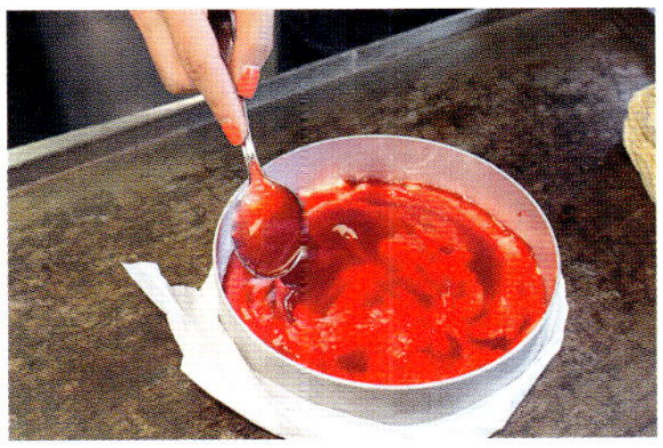

From the ski racer to the cook?

The answer causes a creased forehead. "You know what? You have shown me your cake, now I'll show you my favorite recipe: banana bread!"

Trettl's face shows his surprise. "This has never happened during a session with an athlete. This time it's I who is learning something!" The ingredients are quickly gathered in the kitchen. "The recipe? I bake with my gut feeling, Roland." Roland is shocked: part two. "Lindsey, do you want to start working here? As a cook? Because working with your gut feeling is precisely what differentiates a cook from a patissier. They always take the exact measures as a guideline, not the taste." Even though there won't be an Ikarus cook named Vonn anytime soon, Lindsey the confectioner gets going and in no time mixes bananas, 5 TBSP of sugar, and eggs. She then adds flour and cinnamon, nutmeg, the baking powder, and a pinch of salt, followed by the chocolate chips and the apple sauce. The latter is intended to make the dough juicy, but it can be replaced with butter. Vonn places the dough in a baking tin (those for bread are ideal), adds 2 TBSP of sugar, and puts it into the oven heated to 175 degrees (325°F) for forty-five to fifty minutes. Record time!

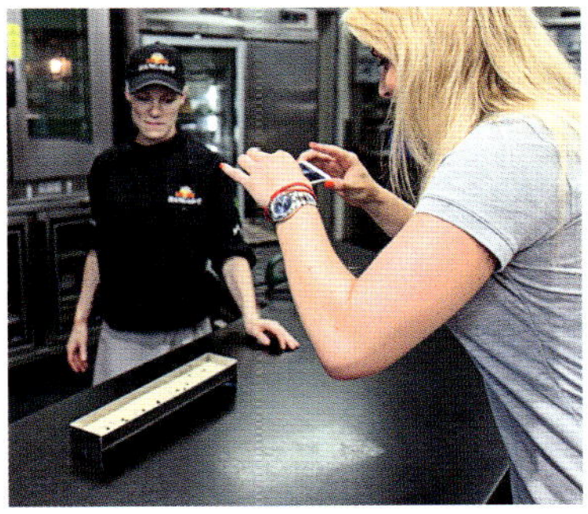

A good sign of quality: the confectioner takes a photo of her creation for posterity.

Less than an hour later, the Linzer cake and banana bread are standing next to each other, ready for a duel. The master confectioner and confectioness carefully sample the still-hot dishes. Lindsey is the first one to break the silence. "Uhm, the banana bread: one of my best ones ever!" And Roland admits with a grin that today he's only good for silver this time around; Lindsey once again takes the lead. The Linzer cake is good, she says. "But it doesn't surprise, and that's what makes for a good cook."

RACECAR DRIVER

AUSTRALIA
RESIDENCE: ASTON CLINTON, UK

MARK WEBBER

NEW GOALS AFTER THE CHECKERED FLAG.

NAME: Mark Alan Webber

BIRTHDAY: August 27, 1976

HEIGHT: 1.85 m (6')

WEIGHT: 75 kg (165 lbs)

DISCIPLINE: Formula 1

HOBBY: outdoor sports

WEBSITE: www.markwebber.com

TWITTER: @AussieGrit

After over 200 Grand Prix victories, Mark Webber ended his career in Formula 1 at the end of the 2013 season ... and left a huge gap in motorsports' royal division. He was a tough but fair pilot who always got the most out of his cars from his sensational debut as number five with Minardi to his victories during the past seven years with Red Bull Racing. And all that while the smart Australian was a latecomer, in that he joined karting at fourteen.

An age when most other talents already have five years of training under their belt. Today, one can safely say that Mark Webber has passed them all, left and right. But the checkered flag at the Formula 1 doesn't mean Webber is about to cut off the engine. Starting in 2014, he began racing for Porsche in the long-distance championship and start of the twenty-four-hour Le Mans.

Devilish: on the Australian island of Tasmania, Mark organizes an extreme sports event, including orienteering, kayaking, mountain biking, and rappelling from an enormous cliff.

2001
2. place Formula 3000 World Championship

2002
1. F1 race (Minardi)

2005
1. Grand Prix podium (BMW Williams)

2009
2 Grand Prix victories (RB Racing)

2010
4 Grand Prix victories (RB Racing)

2011
1 Grand Prix victory (RB Racing)

2012
2 Grand Prix victories (RB Racing)

“Giving up is really not style.”

CHOCOLATE IN HELL.

[INTERVIEW]

HOW TO YOU PREPARE FOR A RACE? WHAT'S ON YOUR PLATE AND IN YOUR GLASS?

Generally speaking, the evening before a race is very important to me, as I don't have any appetite on the day of the race. You're supposed to eat lots of carbohydrates, which is great for me, as I am a huge pasta fan. And there's a strict rule: stay away from seafood.

HOW DO YOU CELEBRATE A SUCCESSFUL RACE?

First champagne, then wine, with my family and best friends around me

WHICH THREE (LIVING OR HISTORIC) PERSONS ARE SITTING AT THE TABLE OF YOUR PERFECT DINNER?

Marilyn Monroe; I am sure she has some good stories to tell. Muhammad Ali, because he is such an inspiring personality. And Princess Diana, because I would have loved to get to know her.

AND WHERE WOULD IT TAKE PLACE?

On a cliff at the edge of the Atlantic Ocean, with a stunning view of the sea.

ARE YOU THE FIRST TO FINISH THEIR PLATE OR DO YOU ENJOY EVERY BITE?

Definitely the first one. Unfortunately I eat way too fast. I should eat much slower, but I probably won't learn that anytime soon.

THE TASTE OF YOUR CHILDHOOD IS ...

... my grandma's chocolate cake. My mother also handles the recipe pretty well.

YOU HAVE ONE LAST MEAL. WHAT DO YOU ORDER?

A lot of chocolate, and then, off into hell. It tastes pretty nice when molten (laughs).

THE LONG WAY TO THE TOP

THE SPAGHETTI KNOT.

How to make spaghetti al dente? The trick of throwing a noodle against a wall is fairly well-known. If it sticks it is supposed to be perfect. Supposedly! "You can't be certain with this method," says Roland. The real expert has a different method: he makes a knot in the tested noodle. "Whether too hard or too soft, the knot will break. Try it out!"

CHILI PASTA

WITH SHRIMP AND CHERRY TOMATOES

20 MINUTES

SCALE 3

INGREDIENTS:
- 2 garlic cloves
- 1 shallot
- 1 chili
- 30 cherry tomatoes
- 600 g (21 oz) spaghetti
- salt
- 150 g (½ cup) olive oil
- 20 fresh shrimp (peeled)
- 1 lime
- pepper
- 1 bunch of rocket lettuce
- Parmesan
- lime zests

Just when he got back from a visit to a future guest cook at the Hangar-7 restaurant, Roland Trettl has to deal with yet another Australian. But the master chef is happy to fight jet lag-induced fatigue for a cooking session with a Grand Prix champion who has accumulated over 200 victories.

But for now Roland Trettl has to be patient, because Mark Webber had to excuse himself for an important meeting.

So Trettl looks over the preparations of Mark Webber's favorite dish: he finely chops the garlic cloves, scallions and the chilis, halves the cherry tomatoes, and puts a large pot of water on the stove.

As if he smelled it, Mark Webber enters the kitchen at that moment. "Sorry for the delay," he apologizes with a jovial hug and presents his fiancée Ann Neal, who has accompanied him to Salzburg to see Roland.

"We're pretty hungry already!"

"Why don't you take a seat meantime," and Roland offers her a seat at the chef's table of Ikarus and turns towards the Formula 1 star: "I think we still have some business to take care of!"

"We're lucky this is a quick dish to prepare," Webber is happy to announce while putting the spaghetti in the pot. "Do we want to add salt?," he asks after a discerning look into the boiling water. "Already taken care of," Roland says, "there's plenty in there."

There's also plenty of olive oil—in the pan, that is—which is now placed on the stove. The scallions, some chili (depending on your taste for spiciness), and the garlic are added. Once the latter is golden-brown, the cherry tomatoes can be added as well and, after a few minutes, the shrimp.

"Don't fry the shrimp for too long, only 1-2 minutes," suggests the master chef. Then, take a scoop of water from the pot with the spaghetti, put it in the pan, and allow it to simmer for a few minutes.

The two of them make use of the short waiting time to talk about the culinary scene down under. "There isn't really a typical Australian cuisine," Webber explains. "Just as the entire country, the cooking is very much influenced by the British. But lately it has become

Empowerment: Mark eats noodles before every race. "But not as spicy, that would be fatal."

more international." "That's true," adds Roland, "funny, I had the best sushi of my life in Sydney, not Japan. All of the large cities offer a great density of excellent restaurants of all kinds of cultures and cooking styles."

Now is the time to direct their attention to Italian cuisine, because the pasta is now perfectly al dente and can be strained with a sieve. It goes into the pan and is mixed with the sauce. A tip from Roland: "If the sauce is too thick simply add a bit of water from the noodles."

He then squeezes one lime over the contents of the pan. "This is for the fresh taste," says the cook of Ikarus before seasoning the dish with salt and pepper and putting it onto the prepared plates. Meanwhile, Mark has chopped the rocket lettuce and puts it over the spaghetti.

"Yeah, that small but important detail!" ...

... enthuses the racecar driver. "I could eat rocket salad with pretty much anything."

The only thing still missing is the Parmesan. "And a bit of lemon zest," says Roland, and grates a bit of lime peel over the finished chili pasta.

"Hey, this looks really great," laughs Mark. "Are you happy as well, Roland?"

"Absolutely! I think we can present it to your fiancée."

QUITTING TIME.

HANNES ARCH

NATASCHA BADMANN

PETER BESENYEI

BJØRN DUNKERBECK

ORLANDO DUQUE

MARKUS EDER

MATTIAS EKSTRÖM

STEFAN GLOWACZ

MARIO GÓMEZ

MARCEL HIRSCHER

MARC JANKO

ROMAN HAGARA & HANS-PETER STEINACHER

KARINA HOLLEKIM

JANA DUKATOVÁ

VAVRINEC HRADILEK

BENJAMIN KARL

OLGA KHARLAN

DAVID LAMA

SERGIO LAYOS

AKSEL LUND SVINDAL

AXEL NAGLICH

MARIANA PAJÓN

GREGOR SCHLIERENZAUER

MARTIN SONKA & MICHAL PROKOP

DANIEL SERRA & FELIPE FRAGA

JORDY SMITH

MARKUS STÖCKL

MATTHIAS TRATTNIG & ALEXANDER BARTA

BEITSKE VISSER

LINDSEY VONN

MARK WEBBER

To those who have created a book from an idea.
Red Bull Creative would like to thank the Ikarus team for their tireless engagement, despite the high-octane daily and festival action. We send a merci to our photographer Georg Wallner, who has actually created the relaxed cooperation between cook and athlete with his almost invisible style of working. For organizational support, a heartfelt thanks to Red Bull Athlete Management, as well as to the management of Hangar-7, Marisa Rubenbauer and Clara Krulich. Robert Blaschke, thank you for your tenacity and the selfless support, without which the "transfer" of Mario Gómez into this book would not have happened. *Ringraziamo di cuore tutto il team del Four Seasons di Firenze per la calorosa ospitalità, in particolare chef Vito Mollica e sous chef Roberto Ceccherini per metterci a disposizione la loro cucina e per il loro generoso sostegno.* And finally, a very special thanks to all the participating athletes, whose enthusiasm and commitment for this project has been simply overwhelming.

Text: Red Bull Creative GmbH, Salzburg; Gernot Hörwertner, Matthias Nelke, Marc Eggers, Lara Soenmezay

Dust jacket/cover design, layout, imprint, lithography: Red Bull Creative GmbH, Salzburg; Karin Wolfsgruber, Grant Coghill, Muhamed Vehabovic, Reinhold Schichtle

Editorial: Dr. Nadja Kneissler; **copy-editing:** Niko Schmidt; **expert advice:** Dr. Stephanie Kloster

PHOTO CREDITS:
Cover: Romina Amato, Philipp Benedikt, Ray Demski, Philipp Forstner, Milan Garth, Jesper Gronnemark, Alberto Lessmann, Damiano Levati, Vitek Ludvik, Tim Lüdin, Nick Muzik, Rutger Pauw, Lukas Pilz, Erwin Polanc, Gerald Rihar, Jarno Schurgers, Jürgen Tap, Bruno Terena, Samo Vidic, Georg Wallner; Getty Images/Red Bull Content Pool

Inside pages: Red Bull Content Pool: Georg Wallner (5, 6, 7, 14, 47, 64, 81, 106, 132, 138, 186, 228, 229, 230 and all cooking photos; except for see Benedikt), Philipp Benedikt (41, 42, 43, 103, 104, 105, 163, 164, 165, 167, 197, 199, 200, 201, 229, 230) (cooking photos by: Orlando Duque, Marc Janko, Matthias Trattnig, Alexander Barta, Gregor Schlierenzauer), Erik Aeder (34), ASP Red Bull (82), Alessandro Belluscio (44), Markus Berger (4, 16), Hamish Blair (156), Thilo Brunner (88), Paulo Calisto (40, 100), Oscar Carrascosa (128), Vincent Curutchet (72), Ray Demski (32, 33, 108), Dutch Photo Agency/Red Bull Contentpool (52, 212), Uwe Düttmann (100), Rainer Eder (120, 122), Andreas Ehrensberger (188), Klaus Fengler (58, 60), Balazs Gard (5, 26, 27, 28, 74), Mirja Geh (4, 22), Renzo Giraldo (146), Jesper Gronnemark (6), Miles Holden (46), Beat Kammerlander (140), Helge Kirchberger (7, 204, 205), Florian Klingler (122), Craig Kolesky (7, 180, 182), Daniel Kolodin (112, 114), Alberto Lessmann (6), Damiano Levati (4), Tim Lüdin (7, 210), Vitek Ludvik (6, 94, 140), Marcelo Maragani (174), Sebastian Marko (154), Ryan Miller (182), Tomislav Moze (38), Rutger Pauw (16, 20, 22, 74, 128), Lukas Pilz (5, 6), Philip Platzer (6, 107), Erwin Polanc (170), Mauricio Ramos (188), Erich Reismann (202), Corey Rich (6, 22), Gerald Rihar (195), Federico Rios (144), Camilo Rozo (146), Andreas Schaad (16, 82), SonStar (34), Erich Spiess (216, 218), John Staples (8), Bruno Terena (168, 174), Mark Thompson (156, 222), Dean Treml (40), Robyn Trnka (152), Luis Vidales (126), Samo Vidic (5, 7, 46, 86, 96, 134, 212), Dan Vojtech (150), Predrag Vuckovic (96), Martin Zilka (94). **Corbis:** New Press Photo/Splash News/Corbis (66) **GEPA Pictures:** GEPA Pictures/Red Bull Contentpool (7, 82, 160, 162, 193), Christian Ort (100), Felix Roittner (196), Harald Steiner (194), Andreas Pranter (196), Christian Walgram (100) **Getty Images:** AFP/Patrik Stollarz (66), Getty Images/Red Bull Contentpool (224, 225), Claudio Villa (66), **Shutterstock:** (115, 147, 103);

Imprint and book cover: Himmer AG, Augsburg

ORIGINAL PUBLISHER'S INFO:
Delius Klasing Verlag, Siekerwall 21, D - 33602 Bielefeld
Tel.: 0521/559-0, Fax: 0521/559-115
E-Mail: info@delius-klasing.de
www.delius-klasing.de

Library of Congress Control Number: 2015947961

Originally published as *Das Athleten Kochbuch* by Delius, Klasing & Co., 2013.
Translated from the German by Jonee Tiedemann

ISBN: 978-0-7643-4966-9
Printed in China

Published by Schiffer Publishing, Ltd.
4880 Lower Valley Road
Atglen, PA 19310
Phone: (610) 593-1777; Fax: (610) 593-2002
E-mail: Info@schifferbooks.com

For our complete selection of fine books on this and related subjects, please visit our website at www.schifferbooks.com. You may also write for a free catalog.

This book may be purchased from the publisher. Please try your bookstore first.

We are always looking for people to write books on new and related subjects. If you have an idea for a book, please contact us at proposals@schifferbooks.com.

Schiffer Publishing's titles are available at special discounts for bulk purchases for sales promotions or premiums. Special editions, including personalized covers, corporate imprints, and excerpts can be created in large quantities for special needs. For more information, contact the publisher.